THE FOUR SEASONS OF RECOVERY

For Parents of Alcoholics and Addicts

How to Help Your Adult Child Give Up Destructive Addictions for Good

Michael Speakman, LISAC

Rite of Passage Press
Phoenix, Arizona

The Four Seasons of Recovery
for Parents of Alcoholics and Addicts
By Michael Speakman, LISAC

Copyright © 2014 by Michael J. Speakman

Published and distributed by:
Rite of Passage Press
P.O. Box 30185
Phoenix, AZ 85046
www.roppress.com

The author of this book does not dispense advice or prescribe the use of any technique as a form of treatment for physical, emotional, or medical problems of any kind without the advice of a physician, either directly or indirectly. The intent of the author is only to offer information of a general nature to help you in your quest for helping yourself and your loved ones find solutions to complex problems. In the event you use any of the information in this book for yourself, which is your right, the author and publisher assume no responsibility for your actions.

SECOND EDITION

Library of congress Cataloging-In-Publication Data

ISBN: 978-1-4951-0079-6

Cover design by Krystina Batt: Tinas@supersigns.com

Printed in the United States of America

DEDICATION

I dedicate this book to all of the wonderful recovering alcoholics and addicts I met in treatment centers. They helped me learn what I needed to know so I could teach parents how to best help their addicted children.

TABLE OF CONTENTS

Introduction..1

How This Book Works...................................... 5
The Seasons of Recovery 5
Additional Helpful Resources 6
Terminology 7
The Stories 7
Magic Moments 8
Disclaimer 8

WINTER 9
How Bad Can it Get?.. 9
Janel's Story... 9
Addict Roles 10
'How Did We Get Here?' 11
The Tennis Court Analogy 12
Sudden Freeze or Gradual Onset? 13
Rose's Story 13
The Game Is Up 15
Magic Moment #1: Committing to Recognizing the Truth.............. 16
Repetitive Winter 16
Janel's Repetitive Winter 17
Hopelessness: A Common Condition For Parents.................... 18
Time for Change 21
Spring Forward 22
The Risk of Change.. 23

SPRING..27
Knowledge is Power 27
Janel Gets Help for Herself 28
Magic Moment #2:
    Committing to Getting New Learning.........................30
Get Help for Yourself 30
Foundations for Progress 31
Parental Guilt..32
The Anatomy of Guilt..32
Sal's Story: Dealing With Guilt and Anger 38
Shifting Your Focus: No Time for Guilt..........................41
How Long Will It Take? 42
When Helping Isn't Helping 42
Enabling Checklist..45
Co-dependency Is Not Healthy Dependency 46
Providing More Precise Help 48
Cardinal Rules for Helping...50
The 'Big Five' Ways to Show Love 56
Childish vs. Childlike
    The Challenges of Delayed Emotional Growth.........58
Delayed Emotional Growth Traits................................64
The Three D's...65
Adult Coping Skills...68
Jackson's Story 69
Drug Addict or Drug Abuser?......................................70
How Old Are You? 73
Parent Roles...76
Through a Parent's Eyes..76
Magic Moment #3:
    Apologizing for Not Treating Your Adult Child as an Adult 79
The Strain on Marriages 80
When There Are Multiple Parents................................83
Janel Takes a Risk...85
Getting Out of Your Comfort Zone 87

Juggling Challenges 88
A Framework: Eleven Principles of Family Education 91
Study and Learn 92
Changing How You Help...98
Magic Moment #4:
    Committing to Changing How You Help 99
Sam's Story 99
Cutting Financial Strings..103
Magic Moment #5:
    Committing to Cutting Financial Strings 104
Financial Strings Checklist 105
How One Mom Explained Cutting Financial Strings to Her Son..107
Developing A Parents' Plan 107
A Parents' Plan for Helping Our Addicted Loved One 109
Why Establish Extreme Consequences? 110
Denise's Story 111
Growth Pain or Wasted Pain? 115
Getting Unstuck 116
Changing Habits Takes Time.. 119
Angela's Story 120
New Parent Roles...123
Recognizing Triggers...124
Playing the Role 126

SUMMER...129
Treatment Options 130
After Treatment Options (Sober Living).....................................131
Janel's Son Gets Help..132
A Long-Term Project...133
Completing Residential Treatment (Rehab) 134
Using Adult Coping Skills...135
Daily and Weekly Recovery Activities...136
Some Sober Leisure Activities..140
Planning for Re-Entry 144

Understanding Aftercare 146
Aftercare Planning 146
Aftercare Plan (Family Agreement) 150
Transitional Living 152
Writing a Recovering Person's Plan 153
Recovering Person's Plan 155
Keep It Simple 156
Life Balance 161
Being Teachable 163
Letting Go 164
Monica's Story 164

FALL 169
Relapse 169
Relapse Triggers 171
Why Relapse Happens 174
The Power of Choice 174
An Addict Is an Addict 175
Addict or Substance Abuser? 176
Total Abstinence 178
What to Do When Relapse Happens 179
Final Financial Help 180
Final Financial Help Agreement 182
Multiple Treatment Attempts 183

NO MORE WINTER 185
Why There's No Going Back 185
Minding Expectations 186
M.Y.E. 186
The 'Hope Hotel' 187
Use Your Team 187
Nuggets: Helpful Sayings for Parents 188
When You're Not in Touch 190

'How Can I Know When I've Done All I Can Do?' 190
Magic Moment #6:
    Experiencing a New Level of Peace..191
Janel Today 191

ADDITIONAL RESOURCES..193
What Do I Do When? 195
Suggested Reading 203
Helpful Organizations 205
What is a PAL Group? 206
How to Start a PAL Group in Your Area 207
The Six Magic Moments 208
Janel's Complete Story..211
About the Author...217
Acknowledgements 219
Index...221

INTRODUCTION

In early 2008, Julie called me to make an appointment to meet with her and her husband, Fred. They had just discovered their nineteen-year-old son Jeff was using heroin.

Once they got over their initial shock, they wondered, "Was it the first time he had used? Or had he been using for years and hiding it?"

At first, Jeff lied about his habit. Then he seemed to be cooperating, but he wasn't providing details about how long he'd been using, why he used, how much he'd been using, and how he saw his future.

"It's no big deal," Jeff told his parents. "It's just like taking pills — all my friends are doing it." Julie and Fred were both devastated, and wondered where they'd gone wrong.

Julie, Fred and Jeff are not alone. According to the National Survey on Drug Use and Health sponsored by the Substance Abuse and Mental Health Services Administration, an estimated 22.5 million Americans aged twelve and older were using illicit drugs in 2011.

Still, Julie and Fred didn't know where to turn. After all, who do you talk to about this sort of thing? And how do you talk about it? They just felt so ashamed.

It will be a long journey for Jeff and his parents as well as any family dealing with a loved one's addiction.

In my more than two decades of working with people and families dealing with substance abuse in group situations, private counseling, and inpatient rehabilitation facilities, I have found it can take years rather than months or weeks for families to work through the issues underlying an addiction. Without addressing these issues, it's difficult, if not impossible, to achieve and maintain sobriety. For most people, doing so is a long-term goal and process.

This book's purpose is to provide realistic hope for parents who may, at times, feel hopeless about trying to help a son or daughter who is addicted to alcohol or drugs. The book is designed to guide them through the disappointment, frustration, and confusion often encountered when trying to help a loved one with addiction problems.

It provides hope gained through new knowledge that is both simple and challenging. Knowledge gained from working with addicts and alcoholics over the last twenty-five years. As you will discover, the book is just a part of your education about this confusing and confounding problem as you continue to learn the best ways to help your addicted adult child.

The book accomplishes its purpose by first providing a simple understanding of the problems of, and solutions to, your adult child's drug and alcohol issues. Once you understand what they need and what they're doing, it's much harder for you to be fooled and much easier to know if they are actually getting help.

Second, the book helps parents of adult children who are addicted to alcohol or drugs by providing a proven, step-by-step plan that provides a framework for family recovery. You get the tools you need to detach and separate from your children. This is not easy and can be emotionally gut-wrenching. Many parents experience a grieving process as their children finally develop their own lives, but seeing them become healthy makes it all worth it.

This book also is helpful for parents with an adolescent child who is drinking or using drugs, and for husbands and wives with spouses who have addiction problems. Additionally, this book may help relatives and friends wanting to help someone with an alcohol or drug problem.

Although the relationship between a parent and a child is different than these other types of relationships, many of the addiction issues — childish behaviors, excessive anger, acting like a victim who needs to be rescued, refusing to take responsibility for decisions, manipulating behaviors, dishonesty — are the same if the person is still active in his or her addiction regardless of age.

For instance, Irene came to a Family Support Group Meeting because her seventy-eight-year-old uncle was finally being treated for alcoholism. Despite his age, her uncle had all the childish characteristics typical of a young adult addict. That's because people can't learn adult coping skills while they are still active in their addiction.

Although many aspects of this book can be helpful to these other types of people, we are focusing on parents of addicted adult children because young people are the largest group coming into treatment today. According to a 2011 study conducted by the National Center on Addiction and Substance Abuse at Columbia University (CASA), substance use by teens is the most significant public health problem in the United States (See *CASAColumbia.org*).

The CASA study found that forty-six percent of all high school students are currently using drugs or alcohol, including nicotine, alcohol, and other drugs, and one in three of those students meet criteria for addiction. The CASA report revealed that ninety percent of adult Americans with addiction began using substances prior to age eighteen.

I chose to write a book specifically for parents of addicts and alcoholics for the same reason I started the Parents of Addicted Loved Ones support group (PAL); because there is no other human relationship like that between a parent and a child. Even though parents have the most power and influence over their children, when addiction enters the picture, the situation mysteriously reverses. Now the child is in the driver's seat. Why does this happen? How does this happen? And more importantly, what can be done about it? These are the questions this book addresses.

The problem of addiction is pervasive and it is challenging, but it can be faced and resolved.

Congratulations on taking a step toward doing so by reading this book.

HOW THIS BOOK WORKS

Much like the seasons of each year, you will face predictable periods as you continue to help your adult child. This book helps you learn about the different twists and turns each "season" offers as you progress. With your commitment to educate yourself, you will make progress.

Most parents say this journey was longer and harder than they expected. It may be because they were going in circles, or it may be because they were actually progressing correctly. But, as you will see, there are many variables, and there are no real shortcuts.

This book is designed to guide your progress. With sufficient education, support, and your willingness to change, you can have realistic hope about the years ahead.

I highly recommend you read the entire book once first. Then you can use it as a reference.

The Four Seasons of Recovery for Parents of Alcoholics and Addicts is organized into the seasons you will go through as you seek to guide your addicted child to live a long and healthy life.

The Seasons of Recovery

There are five basic sections of the book:
1. **Winter** is the cold period of discovering the problem, and the realization that there is much work to be done.

2. **Spring** is a time of hope, when the issues benefit from the sunlight of parent education and understanding, and a plan for helping your loved one get into recovery. It is the largest part of the book.

3. **Summer** is the time when your hope builds because your son or daughter is getting help. Now, you and your adult child are both getting into the rhythm of recovery and creating new and healthy habits.

4. **Fall** is a time most families cannot avoid. It is when the addicted loved one slips back into bad habits, but it does not mean all is lost.

5. **No More Winter** is the promise for the educated family. Armed with new understanding and tools, there is no sliding back to past ignorance and hopelessness.

Additional Helpful Resources

Following the main part of the book are sections with additional helpful information:

- An easy-to-consult guide, "What Do I Do When ...?" to help you as you practice new ways of helping.

- A suggested reading list of books and other information to help you in your journey, as well as a list of organizations that may be helpful.

- More information about what a PAL Group is as well as information on how to start one in your area. PAL is the organization I formed to help parents help each other. Such peer support groups are invaluable for helping you and your loved one. More detailed information is also available on the PAL Web site at www.palgroup.org.

- A complete collection of the Magic Moments, which I'll explain shortly.

- A complete recounting of Janel's story. Throughout the book, you will encounter Janel, a mom whose journey with her son mirrors the seasons of recovery. Because it offers such a clear view of the steps parents go through in their long journey to recovery, I've also offered her story in its entirety.

- An index to help you find the key words and concepts used in this book.

Terminology

Addict: For simplicity's sake, I often use the word "addict" to include alcoholics. Even though alcohol is legal, it is a drug. Technically speaking, all alcoholics are **alcohol addicts** (there is more discussion on the definition of addiction in later chapters).

Drug Use: The term "drug use" includes the use of illegal and also prescription drugs that are being used inappropriately. This is becoming an increasingly serious problem in our society.

Him and her: In referring to your addicted loved one, I refer to "him" or "her," always in that order. This does not reflect any gender bias, but reflects a desire to keep it simple so you can focus on the information.

The Stories

Throughout this book, I use stories to illustrate points. Some stories are composites of actual people and situations I have encountered, but all of the stories are true.

The families and people I have worked with are never mentioned without their permission, and many stories are, sadly similar. If I do refer to actual people, all of their names have been changed to protect their privacy.

Magic Moments

Like mile markers on a freeway, Magic Moments are key milestones that help you measure your progress.

It's important to note your progress because it's easy to feel overwhelmed and lost when trying to help an addicted adult child. When you experience a Magic Moment, it is important to stop and reflect upon your accomplishment.

All Magic Moments can also be seen as a group in the back of the book.

Disclaimer

All of the information in this book is intended to help you think about options and choices, not to suggest a specific action you should take to resolve your or your loved one's problems. You have to make your own decisions and choices.

As I have noted, many families do have similar experiences when facing the challenges of addiction. Even if you are reading books, researching online, and attending support groups (all things I encourage) I cannot emphasize strongly enough the importance of your obtaining professional help for you and for your addicted loved one.

Nothing replaces professional assessment and assistance for your particular situation.

WINTER

"The sky is low, the clouds are mean."
— Emily Dickinson

Winter is that dark time when you discover your adult child's drug abuse problem. Your whole world gets turned upside down, and you ask yourself, "Why has this happened to my child?" You fear that all your hopes and dreams for your son or daughter are dashed. Often, you blame yourself and doubt your parenting abilities. You may not even know where to begin to look for help.

How Bad Can It Get?

Janel's Story

Janel, a single mom and a nurse with two sons, got the shock of her life when she noticed needle marks on her nineteen-year-old son Ernie's arms. "I remember that moment and the flood of emotions that overwhelmed me," recalls Janel.

When he was younger, Ernie had behavioral problems, and Janel had done her best to help him. As a child, he was sent to wilderness camp, and when he got older, he attended boarding school.

With this revelation of Ernie's drug use, Janel knew her worst fears had been realized. She did not know it at the time, but this was to be a long journey for Ernie and her, a journey of hope and of hopes crushed.

Addicts exhibit signs. Sometimes we notice those signs but do not pay much attention to them. Upon confirming that your son or daughter is using drugs or alcohol to excess, it's normal to think back about the signs you were seeing but not paying attention to.

These signs are predictable and can be looked at as roles — addict roles.

Addict Roles
Although we are each distinct individuals, there are common roles addicted loved ones often play when they are in their addiction and also in the early stages of their recovery.

Do you see your loved one acting out any of these roles?

1. **Intimidator** — uses anger to drive people away.

2. **Intellectual** — mistakes knowledge for understanding.

3. **Victim** — blames negative events for their addiction.

4. **Blamer** — blames other people for their addiction.

5. **Dumb bunny** — "I don't understand."

6. **Avoider** — tries to keep a low profile.

7. **Socialite** — keeps a high profile, but is superficial.

8. **A.A. Expert** — speaks in slogans, but doesn't get personal.

9. **Bible Expert** — quotes scripture, but doesn't get personal.

10. **Con Man** — thinks he or she is fooling people.

11. **Know-it-all** — "I know what I have to do."

12. **Magic Fixer** — "I know what caused my addiction."

13. **Skeptic** — "That's a good idea, but it won't work."

14. **Deflector** — tries to focus attention away from him or herself.

15. **Lip Servicer** — agrees to follow through but never does.

16. **Controller** — tries to control the course of his or her recovery.

17. **Rabble-Rouser** — stirs up conflict between people or groups.

18. **Paranoid** — "What will you do with this information?"

Fortunately, each of these roles has proven remedies that a counselor or program can help your loved one with. For you, just recognizing these roles helps you realize that you are dealing with someone who likely needs help.

How Did We Get Here?

Although this is not a book about addiction itself but rather a book for those who have loved ones who are addicted, it may be helpful to understand how a fun-loving kid can get into so much trouble.

Nearly every addict goes through **three stages of addiction**:
1. The **Honeymoon Phase**, when usage is relief from physical and/or emotional pain and/or for pleasure or fun and games.

2. The **Coping Phase**, in which the person "needs" the substance to function even with the normal demands of daily life.

3. The **Desperation Phase**, in which drugs or alcohol become the entire focus of his or her life.

Take Danny, an eighteen-year-old high school senior. His grades were pretty good, and he had been doing very well as a starting pitcher for his school's baseball team. Behind the scenes, however, his increasing use of opiate pain pills and heroin caused him to give up more and more of his normal daily pursuits.

Danny's friends noticed that he increasingly isolated himself, not even returning phone calls as he used to. He drifted away from his friends, then dropped off the baseball team. His routine changed dramatically as he placed more and more focus on making money to buy drugs, hide drugs, and take drugs.

His parents did not notice these changes at first because Danny was so good at maintaining an acceptable front and saying what his parents wanted to hear. He also became adept at not telling the whole truth, avoiding giving them all of the information they wanted.

When his parents first found out about Danny's drug use from one of his friends, Danny was in the *desperation phase.* He had gradually lost so much of his life that the drugs literally were his life.

His mom and dad went to Danny's room and found bits of burned tinfoil (a common sign of heroin "smoking") and noticed that some of his prized possessions were missing. Many of the possessions were later found at a local pawn shop. Wanting to help his son, Dad paid to retrieve Danny's guitar, amplifier and television.

Addicts rarely ask for help until they are in the Desperation Phase. Even then, because they can hide so many of the damaging details, the tip-off to their drug or alcohol use is most often a crisis that alerts parents to a long hidden and growing problem. An addiction usually creeps up slowly, starting as fun, and ending in life-threatening consequences.

The Tennis Court Analogy
When you discover that your adult child is an addict, your roles suddenly change. A useful metaphor is the tennis court example. Imagine you and the rest of your family are on one side of a tennis net, and your addicted son or daughter on the other side with his or her *addiction* standing nearby. (Some people picture the *addiction* as an ugly creature, a devilish character, monster, etc. Feel free to use your imagination here).

It may feel like the family is playing against the addict when the ideal situation would be that the addict and the family are all on one side together, playing against the *addiction*. So it makes sense for parents to say to their son or daughter, "Why don't you come around the net to our side and join us? That way, we can all work together to play against the *addiction* instead of against each other."

This makes perfect sense from a logical standpoint. Unfortunately, the addicted adult child has many reasons (mostly fears) for not simply walking around the net to join the family.

To resolve this dilemma, it can be very helpful for parents and other family members to learn how to make changes in relating to their adult child. This allows family members to move from their position on the court across from their loved one, over to the side of the court near the net. This is a neutral position and are *no longer playing against anyone.*

This is, in effect, meeting your loved one halfway. The theory is that it might be easier for your son or daughter to join you at the net and walk together to your side of the court to play together against the *addiction.*

This metaphor while easy to describe, is not so easy to accomplish. The goal of parent education is to learn the steps necessary to make this complex goal become a reality.

Sudden Freeze or Gradual Onset?

Rose's Story

> *Although she was twenty-seven-years-old and married, Brenda called her mother, Rose, for help when she lost her home to foreclosure.*
>
> *Things had snowballed since Brenda, who had slid into alcoholism, had lost her job because of missing days of work, arriving late, and performing poorly. Making things worse,*

Brenda's husband, Jesse, who was not able to cope with her erratic and irresponsible behavior, had moved out of state to get away from her. Eventually, Brenda ran out of money and friends, and found herself sleeping in her car feeling all alone, desperate, and suicidal.

Fortunately, Rose had previous experience with her husband's alcoholism and had learned the hard way about **over-helping** an addicted loved one. Rose wisely told her daughter that she needed professional help and asked if she was ready to accept it. Brenda did accept help by entering the Salvation Army Adult Rehabilitation Center's six-month program in Phoenix.

For Rose, the arrival of winter was a **gradual onset**. Rose knew Brenda was struggling, but it wasn't until Brenda found herself living in her car that she was ready to accept help.

Unlike Rose, parents who don't know about their loved one's increasing addiction issues experience a **sudden freeze** when they discover their adult child's addiction, usually through a disturbing, unexpected incident.

Most often, a combination of situations through time leads to the moment of certainty. Parents may suspect something is wrong but not be sure what or the extent of the problem.

Often, the addict or alcoholic is so clever at hiding addictive behaviors that family members and friends may only have vague feelings or ideas about the possibility of drug or alcohol abuse but not put any energy into checking it out. We all lead busy lives and can often find other, more comfortable ways to spend our time and energy.

Then later, usually after some stressful situation, that moment of certainty occurs. Many parents think back over time and realize that they "kind of knew but didn't really know," and maybe, honestly, didn't really want to know what was happening.

Whenever the moment of exposure and certainty occurs, it is sad but also can bring a sense of relief. Unlike discovering a loved one has an imminent fatal disease, however, the person who is now informed knows what he or she is dealing with and *that it can be addressed.*

This winter is unlike nature's winter. You know the latter is coming even if you don't know exactly when it will arrive because it comes every year. You have experienced it before and can be prepared.

But how can you be prepared for something this out of context, out of the blue, unexpected, and unwanted? You can't. You can, however, forgive yourself for lack of preparation, and put your energy into getting help for yourself and your family.

The Game Is Up
Getting to that point in life when you say, "The game is up" is key. In so many words, parents need to say to their addicted adult child, "The game is up. I know about your drug (or alcohol) problem, and you know that I know, and I know that you know that I know."

At this point, the truth of the problem is "put on the table" so that everyone can face it and deal with it.

Getting this simple truth out into the open is so important. It must be known so that the addict can get help and the family can finally have a better understanding of the problem and, in many cases, the confirmation of long-held suspicions. The Bible verse, "You will know the truth, and the truth shall set you free", really does apply here.

It does not stop the addict's manipulating behaviors, but it is a marker on the way to recovery for which there is no replacement.

15

For this reason, this time of truth is the first Magic Moment, a pivotal time in your relationship with your adult child.

> **Magic Moment #1: Committing to Recognizing the Truth and Announcing Your Discovery to Your Loved One:**
> *"I know about your problem. I still love you and will do everything I can to get you help to resolve it."*

You and your loved one (as well as any other family members who may be involved, including spouses, partners, their children, grandparents, and others) now are operating from a different baseline. All of you can now proceed from this point of honesty, knowing that there is a problem, and it must be dealt with.

Repetitive Winter

In addition to the sudden freeze or the gradual onset of winter, there is also another aspect of this dark season: **repetitive winter**. Repetitive winter is a function of relapse.

One definition of relapse is "A return to using drugs or alcohol after a period of self-imposed abstinence." Repetitive winter is what parents experience when their son or daughter received some help for addiction, was clean and sober for a while, and then relapsed.

Unfortunately, this can happen multiple times. We call this group of addicts **Relapsers**. Your son or daughter might have spent some time, energy, and money getting help, only to return to using his or her drug of choice or, perhaps, a different one.

There are some individuals who go into treatment for addiction and never experience a relapse because he or she has never had a period of abstinence from all drugs and alcohol with a sincere desire to quit for good. In other words, entering treatment may be the first time they seriously want to be clean and sober. We sometimes call these people **First-Timers**.

There are a fair number of first-timers who enter treatment, but there are also a large number of relapsers entering treatment.

Obviously, there are quite a few parents who have experienced repetitive winter. A goal of this book is to end repetitive winter. Through education, experience, and the willingness to make small incremental changes in how you help your addicted son or daughter, you will be able to get to a point in your life where you no longer experience the winter of recovery.

When relapses occur, however, you may experience that old, familiar hopeless feeling again, but it will only be temporary and not your way of life as it was before. It is temporary because you now know what to do or you know where to go to find out what to do. This is the promise of your commitment to education and new action when helping your adult child.

The reason you have experienced repetitive winter is because you moved on from winter by achieving some hope when your addicted son or daughter got help for his or her addiction. You went right back into winter, however, when your loved one relapsed.

In other words, they "went into recovery" for a period of time, and you could experience your adult child getting healthy and feeling better. But how long did that last? Was it a brief respite from winter? Was it a long breather?

Janel's Repetitive Winter
As Janel's story continues, although Ernie had been in rehab several times for his opiate addiction, by age twenty-

six, Ernie had yet to show a consistent desire for recovery. Like so many parents with this problem, Janel had lived a roller-coaster-like life because of Ernie's erratic attempts to get help.

Each time, however, she knew that she was better off than she had been before she began educating herself. She remained consistent in how she interacted with Ernie despite his relapses.

As you will see in our next chapter, the season of spring is when *you* get help, education, and support. Without such knowledge about recovery from addiction, you could be fooled into false hope multiple times.

Spring is that time when you make the commitment to learn what you need to learn to help your adult child better. Your loved one may still relapse, because you don't have any control over that. And you may briefly go into winter as a result, but with the knowledge gained from your time spent during spring's learning time, winter will not be the same long-term, hopeless abyss it might have been.

Eventually, through time of education and experience, the promise is "No more winter".

Hopelessness — A Common Condition for Parents
For an addicted loved one's parents, the shock of the situation and then the often frustrating continued drug or alcohol use ("Why won't he or she stop using these drugs?" "How can he or she not know what the risk is?") can lead to hopelessness, the feeling that you are on an endless treadmill of despair. This is especially true if you are approaching it in a way that does not lead to resolution.

Hopelessness is the hallmark feeling of the season of winter. When it comes to helping your addicted adult child, the way you know you are in winter is that you feel hopeless. You now are on the road to gaining hope, but for right now, a sense of hopelessness is all too common and to be expected. It is a complex issue, but one you can address.

Part of the reason for hopelessness is that you find yourself in the middle of something that you do not understand, causing you to feel overwhelmed. The situation often began without you, and you can't see an end in sight, so resolution seems impossible, especially if your loved one is not eager to address his or her problem.

Your hopeless feeling from your adult child's drug or alcohol use or relapse may occur, but how long must you feel that way? Even though this painful feeling negatively affects every aspect of your life, ask yourself, "How long must I feel this way?"

Further, ask yourself, "Do situations or other people have complete control of my feelings, or do I have a measure of control over my own hopeless feelings?"

Asking yourself these questions, answering them truthfully, and embracing them may help parents realize there is a way out.

What if your hopelessness comes not just as a result of your adult child's drug or alcohol use or relapse, but also because of your lack of education about recovery from addiction? Not having the knowledge or resources necessary to deal with this complex and emotional situation can lead to a predictable cycle of hopeful expectations when your son or daughter is getting help, then a sense of hopelessness when he or she relapses.

Feeling hopeless is a *learned* condition, not a natural condition. Hope is a human beings' natural condition. After all, have you ever met a baby who feels hopeless? To feel hopeless, you must believe that your loved one's life will never get any better. What type of situation do you imagine would have to happen for a parent to be headed down the road known as the **Hopeless Highway**? And, how long would the situation have to persist to arrive at the point of hopelessness?

It depends upon the people involved and their individual experiences, but prolonged and repeated relapse can put you on this ruinous road.

Hopelessness *can* be replaced with hope. It's done by turning around and heading the opposite direction on that highway; one you didn't, after all, ask to be on. Even though your hopeless feeling can be changed through education, you must take the **risk of trusting** other people to help you make that U-turn toward hope.

This would be an ideal time to get help for yourself. It just makes good sense for you to see a counselor who understands addiction and recovery and who can help you cope with all the stress you have been carrying. It's important to note that getting such help for yourself will end up benefiting your addicted son or daughter in powerful ways that may not be obvious.

In general, to remain hopeless, people must cut off meaningful communication with others. That is, keeping true thoughts, feelings, innermost needs, and desires secret, rather than revealing them to another person who could help. That other person helps by providing a fresh and objective perspective.

Many times "the hopeless among us" are easy to spot because they are obviously cutting off communication by isolating themselves. Interestingly enough, though, a hopeless person might also be the most outgoing one in the room, yet remain at a surface level in all of his or her communication.

The hopeless person is actually remaining so by:

1. Not revealing a need for help.
2. Not asking for help.
3. Not accepting help from others.

All three of these hidden problems must be overcome if someone is to make the journey from hopeless to hopeful. Hope can be restored when a hopeless person takes the risk of revealing his or her need for help to someone outside himself or herself, whether it is another person or a higher power.

This type of **self-revealing** requires taking a big personal risk. "What if the person to which I tell my *deeper truths* thinks less of me, or makes fun of me, or tells others about me?"

What might help motivate a hopeless person to take the scary risk of self-revealing? Or what could help him or her reduce the risk of self-revealing? The answers to such questions can help us understand how we might better help the hopeless return to being hopeful.

Ironically, a person often must feel hopeless enough to take that risk. As the author *Anais Nin* once wrote, "The day came when the risk to remain tight in a bud was more painful than the risk it took to blossom." Once someone is willing to take the risk, that's where *people-helpers* like counselors or a good friend may come in. They are there when a person who needs help finally has the courage to ask for assistance.

Time for Change

When you first find out that your loved one has an addiction problem, it can be as much of a shock as finding out that someone you love has contracted a terminal illness.

In fact, your emotional state is not unlike one you might feel if someone you loved passed away. As one mother said to me recently,

"When my son admitted he was using heroin, it felt like he just told me he was going to die." In other words, you may feel a mixture of sadness, anger, fear, guilt, and shame.

Whether you just found out yesterday or have been dealing with this problem for twenty-five years, the time comes when you realize that something has to change. The word "realize" can be defined as "to make real in your experience." Sometimes parents of addicted loved ones knew in their hearts that something wasn't right, and now it is time to come to terms with it intellectually and deal with it appropriately.

If you've been dealing with an addicted loved one for a while, you've probably noticed that, no matter how much you keep trying to help, you realize (there's that word again!) that perhaps what you have been doing may not be working, at least not in any long-term or progressive way.

The simple or sometimes not so simple acceptance that you have a problem that requires the help of another person is a huge step forward because it acknowledges that you, as a parent, are not able to help your child by yourself. Although you may experience some shame and guilt initially, you are finally on your way to having the healthy family relationships you have longed for.

Spring Forward
At a certain point, it becomes obvious that winter must pass and spring is the season you can now embrace.

Even if your son or daughter is not yet getting help, *you can get help for yourself*. The long, slow process of getting used to focusing on yourself, your feelings, your needs, your problems, your solutions, etc. comes from practicing it.

At certain points, it's more important to focus on *you* than on your son or daughter. And even though it's a slow and indirect strategy, getting help for yourself does work and will ultimately end up helping your adult child more than you can imagine. Parents have repeatedly told me that the rewards of this action outweigh all the effort necessary.

This new way of thinking, in which you are focusing on you instead of him or her, does not come naturally to parents. After all, you have been caring for this person all of his or her life.

Even though he or she is now legally an adult, you may find that you have given the majority of your time and energy over the past many years to your addicted son or daughter.

It might be time now to begin exploring such thoughts as "Have I shortchanged any of my other children? My spouse? My work? My friends? And, most important, myself?"

Initially, you might feel guilty about this neglect of others in your life. You may have been, or feel you have been, shortchanging other people while you focused the bulk of your energy, time, money, and other resources on someone who not only doesn't always seem to appreciate it, but someone who continues to act in self-destructive ways and, perhaps, continues to spiral downward despite your commitment and sacrifice.

As you become educated about the situation you are in, you will see why you can put these thoughts and feelings behind you so you may all move into a more promising future.

The Risk of Change
The first payoff from your courage to get helpful education on addiction and recovery comes quickly: you now have fresh hope for your son or daughter, for yourself, and for your family as a whole. Then, as

your courage increases, you can take some baby steps to help your loved one.

But you must first learn about the approaches and guidelines that will help you take this different path with your addicted loved one.

The focus is on you.

If you have had hopes before and had them dashed repeatedly, rest assured that this time is, indeed, different. Hopelessness usually comes from basing your hope on your loved one's willingness to change *instead of your own*.

This is especially frustrating because you know you've been helping him or her every way you know. And yet, how has it worked? As Albert Einstein once said, "Insanity is doing the same thing over and over again and expecting different results."

At PAL meetings, we often remind each other:

"This is a marathon, not a sprint."

We may not reach the finish line quickly, but we will reach it nonetheless.

As a family member, you will learn things that you didn't even know you needed to learn. Your education will come from books, counselors, and, in particular, support groups.

These groups not only provide support, they also offer educational opportunities, encouragement, and prayer from people going through the same things you are. When you see and hear the situations, fears, and concerns you share with others, you will not feel so alone.

A support group, however, cannot substitute for the intangible gifts you receive from a good counselor or life coach. I believe it's important to find a counselor or coach who is educated about and experienced with addiction, co-dependency and grief issues.

The process of family education is similar to a person taking a series of community college courses. These courses may take a couple of semesters, and in some cases, anywhere from six months to two years to complete. Your education is a long-term process because you will be learning new things and putting your new learning into practice.

Your education will bolster both your intellectual understanding and the practice of new behaviors. Some good news, though: this is not like continuing education. You don't have to go to school forever.

Yes, you will continue to learn life lessons until the day you leave this world, but when it comes to healing addiction, you can learn enough in six to twelve months to create a **foundation of new knowledge**.

You'll know you've achieved this foundation when, no matter what your loved one does, you will either know what to do or you will know where to find out what to do.

As you learn more, you will discover that your new skills will also carry over into the rest of your life in a positive way. You will be able to use the skills you learn with other people, creating a healthy and more mature way of communicating with others.

For all the changes your addicted loved one must make, and there are many, the first place change must take place is with you, the only person you truly can change. You must make a commitment to change your own beliefs, habits, and actions. Until you do, the same cycles will simply repeat.

You are not making these changes alone or blindly, though. You will have many sources of support, including this book, counselors, groups, and other parents who are taking a similar journey.

You are also armed with a new awareness and new tools to help you.

This time, it's different.

This "formula" is an easy way to see why:

Change = awareness + new action

Now you are equipped with a new awareness that helps you know why you must do and say something different than you have been doing and saying. Now you will also have a framework to do so.

It's time to ask yourself, "Am I willing to change?"

For you to succeed, the answer must be "Yes."

SPRING

"For the winter is past and the rain is over and gone.
The flowers are springing up
and the time of singing birds has come."
— Song of Solomon 2:11-12

Spring is a time of hope. You have found help for yourself, whether it's in a book, a group, a treatment center, counseling, or some combination thereof. You are not alone anymore, and you can feel a sense of comfort knowing that.

You have fresh hope that things can now really change for the better.

Knowledge is Power
The field of substance abuse counseling is complex and confusing, but it's not unknown. In this field, we know that there is a *set of known variables*, and we know all of those variables.

We also know that your addicted loved one has other problems in addition to drug and alcohol abuse, but they are not problems we have never seen before. There seems to be an unlimited number of problems associated with addiction: excessive anger, inability to learn from mistakes, dishonesty, self-destructive behaviors, relapse, legal problems, physical problems, domestic problems, emotional problems, spiritual problems, and on and on. Yes, the list is long and it is to be expected, because addiction affects every area of a person's life.

27

Fortunately, not only do we, in the recovery field, know all the problems, we also know all the solutions to the problems. Your adult child cannot have a problem for which we don't have a solution.

That's because there is a curriculum for recovery, which can provide realistic hope, and that is what you are learning here.

It is not necessary for you to learn every detail about addiction and recovery from addiction. It will be extremely helpful for you, however, to gain an *overview* of addiction and recovery from addiction, and that will be your foundation for being able to make new and more effective decisions when helping your loved one.

You'll get that overview as you educate yourself through time about these issues. Like calculus, you can't learn it all at once, but one morning you wake up and realize you truly understand it.

Janel Gets Help for Herself

At this point in her story, Janel is ready to get help, but this time for herself. The first time Janel came to a family support group, she looked stressed and lost, but she was listening and open to sharing her thoughts and her true feelings. In a word, she was participating.

Janel shared with the group that she thought all she had to do was to get her son into Calvary's thirty-day rehab program and everything would be fine. He would come out after a month, and all of the problems he'd always had would be taken care of.

She laughs at herself now when talking about this, but back then that is how she truly felt. This expectation explains her deep disappointment when Ernie not only left treatment early on his own against staff advice and went back to using drugs, he also went back to the drug-using girlfriend with whom he was in a co-dependent relationship.

Janel was happy when she was able to talk Ernie into going back and completing his program at the Calvary Addiction Recovery Center. Then he left treatment early again, however, this time because he was asked to leave the center for severe misconduct. And once again, he returned to the drugs and the girlfriend.

Janel reported that she was tired of the roller-coaster ride of feeling great when Ernie was getting help and then deeply depressed when he relapsed.

As a healthcare professional herself, she smiled when she said, "I think I've become bipolar because of my son!" Finally, Janel was ready to learn how to help Ernie without enabling him.

She did not know it at the time, but she soon discovered that she could accomplish that goal. Sure, it would take time, but not an unreasonable amount of it. More importantly, she learned that it was possible, and she wanted to do it. This was the beginning of her discovery of hope.

Janel was entering spring. She was ready to commit to taking the action steps necessary to understand recovery from addiction, knowing that she needed to learn more before she could ever be truly helpful to Ernie over the long haul.

Making this decision, and letting your loved one know you have made it, is an important step in creating a healthier relationship with him or her. You are going to have new knowledge that lets you interact with your adult child differently, and he or she will know soon that this is so. You are moving ahead, and everyone will know it.

Now that you have made the decision to change, you have committed to educate yourself. Letting your adult child know you are doing so is your next pivotal moment.

Magic Moment #2: Committing to Getting New Learning and Letting Your Loved One Know You Are Doing So:
"I'm educating myself in order to help you better."

For instance, one mother said to her son, "You may have noticed some changes in how your dad and I treat you and help you. If you haven't, you will, because we are committed to learning how to help you better."

Get Help for Yourself

Fortunately, you do not need to face this problem alone. This is the time to reach out for help from other people who know what you're going through.

Help is available from experts in the field of addiction and also from other people facing the same issues as you. There are self-help groups such as PAL (Parents of Addicted Loved ones), the group I started for parents in 2006. There are also well-established organizations for family members such as Al-Anon (for family members of alcoholics); Nar-Anon (for family members of addicts); and Families Anonymous. You can find information about all these groups in the back of this book and a lot more information about each on the Internet.

This is also the time to consider the benefits of counseling for yourself. It is often quite helpful at this point to arrange a session with a substance abuse counselor who can help you make decisions based on his or her professional experience and knowledge.

Finding a counselor who is right for you and your situation can be done online, through recommendations from friends and/or family, by calling treatment centers, or by asking other members of self-help groups.

Driven by guilt, shame, and pride, at this point many people feel it might be best to keep the problem in the family. They hope to protect their family's name or think they may be able to "fix" it themselves. These are some of the most common thoughts and feelings that occur as winter dawns.

The chances that avoiding professional assistance will succeed in your loved one getting help and resuming a normal life are, unfortunately, slim. Many parents who try this route find themselves spiraling down into depression and bankruptcy as they try unsuccessfully to help their adult children in a way that ends up not actually helping.

Other parents have been through these challenges before you and they, as well as seasoned professionals, can help you. You are not alone in this season, nor the ones that follow. Once you make the decision to abandon the notion of going it alone, your hopelessness begins to give way to hope.

Foundations for Progress
The first principle of the PAL Group is *recovery from addiction has a curriculum and you can learn it.*

The second major principle of PAL is that in most cases, your son or daughter, in addition to being addicted, is also suffering from *delayed emotional growth.* We'll talk more about this very important issue.

Part of what you will learn is how to help your addicted loved one more constructively. This is good for him or her and good for you, as it stops the merry-go-round of actions that you thought would help but often perpetuates the destructive behavior.

Parental Guilt

Feeling guilty is a common problem that most parents with an addicted child experience. It's very normal for parents to ask themselves such questions as:

"Where did we go wrong?"

"What should we have done differently?"

"What did we do to cause this problem?"

Through education you will learn that you most likely did the best you could given what you knew at the time.

There is a saying about your loved ones and their addiction that is attributed to Al-Anon and referred to as "The Three C's":

- *You didn't Cause it;*
- *you can't Control it;*
- *and you Can't cure it.*

You can, however, educate yourself in such a way that you can help yourself and your addicted loved one from here on.

The Anatomy of Guilt

Guilt is a natural feeling that comes to you when you feel you have done something wrong. For instance, most people feel guilty about lying to a friend for their own convenience. If, in your model of the world, lying is against your moral code, then you will feel guilt.

Guilt can be compared to a pain that urges you to take some remedial action. For example, let's say you admit to a friend that you lied to him. The remedial action is that you sincerely say you're sorry, and then ask for his forgiveness.

This is how you get rid of the pain of guilt; you *take a right action that makes up for your wrong action.*

Surprisingly, guilt isn't all bad. With **true guilt**, which is also called healthy guilt, you can see the wisdom of the emotion. For example, let's say you knew that you had a bald tire on your car and neglected to have the tire replaced. That tire blew, and you had an accident. At that point, you know that the accident was your fault, and you decide to never, ever ignore a bald tire again.

You have learned from the experience. Now you can keep what you have learned and move on, shedding the true guilt; you don't need to feel bad about the situation anymore, because *you have learned the lesson.*

True guilt helps you know when you've done something wrong and provides pain to motivate you to do what's right. And that's the key point: *once you do what is right, the pain goes away.*

What if you have guilt that does not go away? Either:

- You have some amends to make with people to get rid of your true guilt, or

- You haven't learned the lesson available to you through your experience, or

- You're experiencing the all-too-common **false guilt**. This is also sometimes called unhealthy guilt.

False guilt is just as painful as true guilt, but trickier to get rid of.

True guilt can be released by making amends. False guilt, however, is not based on something bad you did knowingly, so you can't make amends. Once again, "knowingly" is the operative word here. Fortunately, you can address this issue through counseling.

Some years ago, I had a personal opportunity to suffer false guilt. I enjoyed, on occasion, taking my son out to dinner to enjoy a good steak. We enjoyed the chance to get together and have a good dinner.

About that time, my son began experiencing pain in his midsection. Through a process of elimination, the doctors determined that both of his kidneys were failing. The doctors never found the cause, but he eventually needed and received a kidney transplant.

I knew that eating protein was hard on your kidneys and I could have felt guilty after enjoying numerous, meat-heavy meals with my son, but we had no way of knowing at the time that it could make his health problems worse. Because I was familiar with the concept of false guilt, I knew better than to feel guilty about a problem I had known nothing about.

How does this apply to addiction? Let's say you gave your addicted son some money and didn't know he was going to buy drugs or alcohol with it. You should not feel guilty for giving him the money, because you didn't know he was going to use it to buy drugs or alcohol.

This could become an open door for false guilt, however, if maybe days, weeks or years later you learn that giving him money was not the best way to help your son. Then, upon hearing this new information, you go back in time in your mind and pretend that you knew then what you know now and feel guilty for enabling your son to become an addict even though you had no idea what you were doing.

Do you see the mind trick here that we humans sometimes play on ourselves? I believe false guilt is one the most common sources of emotional pain because it is so easy to accept when you are operating in the vacuum of private shame.

Since you can't go back in time and undo the error you made back then, you are stuck with false guilt until you confront it. You can't get rid of false guilt by making amends, because you didn't *knowingly* do anything wrong.

Counseling helps you sort out your false guilt from your true guilt, making this a good topic of discussion between you and your counselor.

When all of your true guilt is clear in your mind, you have a roadmap for actions to take to get rid of *all* of your guilt.

What if you got rid of your false guilt first, then dealt with your true guilt? This approach makes more sense, because for many people, false guilt can be so vast and expansive that it can hide true guilt (because it all mixes together in our minds) making it difficult to deal with either.

Just having the intellectual knowledge that false guilt is false does not get rid of it. You must take some kind of action demonstrating your commitment to stop carrying it around. Theoretically, it should be much easier to get rid of false guilt, because no new action, such as making amends and asking for forgiveness, is required. Our complex human minds, however, can make getting rid of false guilt harder than getting rid of true guilt.

False guilt can be released by talking with someone you trust, like a counselor, who helps you sort through your thinking, identify false guilt, and release it. Ritual or ceremony can also be very helpful here. You can pursue these approaches with your counselor, your sponsor, a spiritual advisor, on your own, with a spouse or friend, or any combination thereof.

Also, many people have used prayer to release their false guilt because all it requires is their willingness to let it go. No new action is required, but a change of thinking is required, a change based on having greater understanding of a complex problem.

If you are letting go of your false guilt through the method of prayer, it might be wise to ask God to only take half of your guilt first. That's because removing all of your false guilt too soon can be a big shock. It's amazing how used to something we can become because of habit and time.

We can get used to an excessive amount of emotional suffering before we take action. Having so much guilt removed so quickly can actually feel dismaying and confusing because we can become so accustomed to negative feelings such as guilt that we have an unconscious desire to hang on to them.

Why would you hang on to them? These negative feelings are what is known to you, and the known is almost always easier to accept than the unknown, even if what is known is truly awful. The security that comes from familiarity, even familiar pain, can be more acceptable than the scary unknown.

In some cases, perhaps forgiving yourself for carrying around so much of this false guilt for so long might be in order.

Be aware, too, that when you release all of your false guilt, your true guilt will come into clear view. This might be unsettling initially, but now that you can see it clearly, you'll be able to see and take the steps you need to shed your true guilt as well. Stop for a moment and think: how would it feel for you to be eventually guilt-free?

A good counselor can help you sort through this. No human being can deal with his or her emotions alone. This is the lesson I learned at age thirty-six when I "hit bottom" and attempted suicide. That attempt scared me enough to sincerely ask for help and listen to a good counselor who began to help me understand my emotions and my emotional pain. As it turned out, guilt was a large part of that pain.

A counselor is also a tremendous help if it's unclear to you whether your guilt is justified or not. I believe this is impossible to do alone. And remember, now you are no longer alone.

Working on your guilt issues, especially if they are severe and intense, is a very important step as you help your addicted child. Working on your guilt about your son's or daughter's addiction does not mean that you will lose your motivation for helping your loved one. It does, however, raise the issue of how much of your *help* is motivated by your guilt.

Counseling and support groups can assist you with this common issue because they help you see more clearly how your addicted loved one uses guilt to manipulate you.

Guilt and anger comprise much of the emotional pain that comes as a result of your adult child's problems. At times, it can seem to have no boundaries and can ebb and flow like the ocean beating against the shore.

Another painful issue is the fear of your loved one being found dead somewhere. That is a difficult issue and a painful one for anyone to deal with, but it won't go away by not talking about it.

In general, you can reduce the intensity of your fears by communicating them to someone you trust enough to discuss your deepest feelings with. This could be a friend, family member, or counselor.

This fear, every parent's worst nightmare, also has an often hidden, darker side: it can be used by your son or daughter to manipulate you. In fact, you might have already experienced this. Whether your addicted loved one is doing this consciously is secondary to the fact that this awful possibility is often used by addicts to get what they want, because they will do anything to get it.

Some parents have dealt with this issue, sometimes with the help of a counselor, sometimes just with communicating with their Creator. The most efficient way of reducing the impact of that horrible pain, of what might or could happen is to face it and work on accepting the reality of it.

Sal's Story: Dealing With Guilt and Anger
Sal, a father of an eighteen-year-old heroin addicted daughter, told me how he dealt with the fear of all the grief, guilt, shame, and anger he would feel if she died of an overdose of drugs. Here is Sal's story:

Between the ages of fifteen and twenty-two, my daughter went through a very difficult time. It was, without question, the most difficult thing my wife and I had faced in raising our children. It was every father's nightmare ... and was creating enormous strain and tension in our household, our marriage, and in my heart.

Over time, in trying my best to deal with all the problems and issues, and not succeeding at all, I found I was very angry. I'm talking about anger I had seldom experienced with the exception of a "flare up" or two which soon "cooled off" and my temperament returned to normal, whatever that is. This was different. It was unrelenting. There seemed to be no relief at all, which only made the anger worse. I became afraid of my own thoughts and the possibility of what I might actually do, should I lose control, which seemed to be a growing possibility.

It was clear my daughter had some problems, serious ones, but what was also becoming clear is that I had some problems ... and they were serious, as well. Through a long night of struggle and prayer, one of the richest times of conversation I have ever had with God, I became convinced that my daughter was acting like a fifteen-year-old... and so was I. I needed to change. I needed to take my eyes off her, and pay attention to my own life, my own heart.

Over time, I began to realize my anger was fear based. My fear was raging out of control, and so my anger was raging out of control. The fear I faced was not complicated and was based on two objects. The first was that I believed my daughter was going to die if she continued on the path she was walking; it was that simple. I believed it; I was certain of it. This is one of the greatest fears a parent can face, and will lead to much anger and extreme behavior. I had to face this fear head-on and understand that I could not control my daughter's life or keep her alive if she chose otherwise. I was not in control of my own life, much less hers. I had to give her to God, and let her live her life, with the trust that God alone could save her.

Fortunately, something helped me to face this fear. I imagined the worst scenario I could think of: she died, and I was at her funeral. I was able to vividly imagine this, even feeling the horribly painful emotions of that moment. I saw myself approach her coffin and looking down on her body. I then spoke to her, "I miss you so much, and I love you more than you could ever know." I reached a sort of imaginary closure with this possibility.

Within days, I found the opportunity to reveal this to my living daughter. I told her, "I am afraid that you are going to die, and it is just so hard for me to watch, I can't stand it. But I know that your life is yours to live, it is not mine to control. I want you to know that I have come to grips with this possibility [I explained the imagined funeral], and I also want you to know that I love you more than you can imagine, and I always will. Nothing you ever do will stop me from loving you; of this I am now certain."

The other object of my fear was actually harder to uncover, and far more ugly. To fear for my daughter's life was noble; what good father would not fear this? But the ugly truth is that I also feared for myself, for the experience of pain I would feel, for the embarrassment of being revealed as a lousy dad, a lousy husband, and admit the truth of it. How could I think this way? What sort of selfish heart is this? Why was I so afraid of being revealed and possibly being rejected? This was a hard glimpse into a dark place in my heart.

Again, I had to face this fear head-on. I had to prayerfully admit and confess that I was not a good dad, but a man who had a ton of issues and had made a ton of mistakes. I turned to God for forgiveness and accepted that other people, some quite close to me and some whose opinions mattered a great deal to me, may well reject the real me.

I had to come out of hiding and face the reality of my life and my situation. I had to learn how to love my daughter without regard for my image, my hopes, my dreams and my expectations. I had to love her unconditionally, as God loves me. I am who I am, and that is not a pretty picture on many days, but with the help, love and acceptance of God, I am going to love my daughter, no matter what.

If some don't accept me, or like me, or believe I am acting like a good father would act, I'm okay with that. Before God, I have only one job to do with my daughter and that is to love her, starting now.

In facing my fears directly, and letting God show me how to deal with them, I found an amazing thing: my raging anger went away. Love had room to grow, and it did. I also found the freedom to be real, to share openly with others, and to let others think as they will. I am not in control of anyone else ... Thank God.

The burden of excessive false guilt can make it more difficult than necessary to learn the best ways to help your adult child. It can feel like dragging around a bag of rocks while you're running a marathon. You will continue on this journey to learn how best to help your son or daughter, and many times it will actually mean helping your loved one less. *More is less in many situations.*

You can see the challenge of being able to use this new wisdom when you're carrying around too much guilt, so addressing guilt is a key to being able to help yourself and your addicted loved one.

What would it feel like to be guilt-free for even one hour?

This is something you can look forward to as you sort through your guilt and resolve it, and learn how to address such situations as they come up in your future.

Shifting Your Focus: No Time for Guilt

Focusing on yourself instead of your son or daughter may feel foreign and may even feel selfish enough to produce guilt. But often you must take this step first to escape the hopelessness of winter that you may be deeply mired in, especially if your son or daughter is not quite ready for help.

That's because *you* are ready for help. The actions you take to get help such as *going to meetings, seeing a counselor, reading books, and practicing new behaviors when relating to your adult child* can make all the difference in the world.

Focusing on yourself can be the difference between a hopeless winter and the hope of spring, especially if you communicate to your addicted adult child, "I'm getting help for me no matter what you do."

How Long Will It Take?
Remember, spring is that time in the seasons of recovery when you are getting help even though your loved one is not. Summer marks the time of your son or daughter getting some help for him or herself.

Due to circumstances beyond your control, you can find yourself in spring for a long time. This is because your son or daughter, not you, will determine how long he or she avoids help. Your continued education in spring can, however, help shorten your loved one's avoidance of help.

That's because putting into practice what you are learning will make it harder for you to be manipulated. There is less chance, therefore, of you unintentionally feeding a loved one's addiction.

When Helping Isn't Helping
Once you acknowledge your loved one has a problem, it is good to remember that this is your adult child's problem, not your problem. Nonetheless, you have a part in the process of his or her recovery.

I would never suggest you ignore or abandon your addicted loved one, even temporarily. You need to take action as soon as possible, but what action? That is the question you face over and over again on this journey, a passage that is unwanted and unknown but is nonetheless yours.

There is a lot of confusion in our society about the best way to help our loved ones. It's very easy to **over-help** an adult child. One of the challenges is not being aware that you might view your son or daughter as helpless and needing you and believe he or she cannot get along without you. It is very common to think this way about adolescents who will soon legally become adults when they reach eighteen.

Will their parents still help them financially as if they are still adolescents? Or will the parents adjust their thinking process and treat their children who are over eighteen as adult children? This is not just a trivial point, but it is often overlooked in our society, and can be the root cause of many harmful enabling behaviors.

Although unseen, this perspective communicates to the adult child the notion that "I am helping you because you cannot help yourself." Of course this is never really said out loud, but it remains in the dark, hidden realm of the individual person's thought process and is often part of a parent's reality.

It is very helpful for parents to realize they might be unintentionally helping their loved ones remain stuck on *his or her* side of the *net*. (Remember the tennis court metaphor?)

Until parents get educated about dealing with an addicted loved one, they sometimes play both sides of the court. When life puts the ball (a problem) in their son or daughter's court, so to speak, then mom or dad jumps over the net and hits the ball back (solving the problem) for their adult child. After doing so, he or she then jumps back over the net and returns to their normal position of playing against his or her loved one. That is not only confusing, it's exhausting for everyone involved.

One of the most common but not always immediately noticeable problems is that you may try to help your addicted loved one the same way you would help someone who doesn't have an addiction.

For example, if your daughter had diabetes, you would not help her the same way you might help another family member who does not have diabetes. If she asked you for a box of donuts, you probably would not give them to her. But if her brother, who does not have diabetes, asked for donuts, you might provide them.

Now, suppose your daughter asks for money and you suspect she is going to buy donuts with it. What would you do? If she was upset when you said "No," would you stick to your position? What if your daughter says, "You gave my brother donuts. Do you love him more?"

There is some middle ground between the all-or-nothing strategy of helping a loved one and giving no help at all. Sometimes called **healthy helping**, this middle ground is more an art than a science. It is art that can be learned, one that you are learning by reading this book and taking the steps you need to educate yourself.

The paradox is that, in order for addicts to seek help for their addictions, they need the pain from the consequences of their addiction to be stronger than the relief they get from using the drugs or alcohol.

This puts a double-bind on the parents whose job is to save their children from pain. You can see the tremendous pressure parents can feel when, in their minds, their nineteen-year-old son for instance, is acting like a twelve-year-old child, and the parents respond by taking care of him as if he were twelve.

No consequences, no pain. No pain, no need to change. Parents are constantly asking me, "Why does he still do this?" and I most often answer, "Because he can." This is where the sticky problem of **enabling** comes in. Although you want to help, enabling means you are actually helping someone continue in his or her addiction, which is the opposite of your intention. It may seem like you are helping your loved one in the short term, but you are not helping him or her long term.

Enabling Checklist

How do you know if you are enabling? Read through these questions and answer each one for yourself:

1. Have you ever covered a financial debt that is the result of behavioral dysfunction or drug or alcohol use?
2. Have you ever called to cancel an appointment on someone's behalf because of his or her dysfunctional behavior?
3. Have you ever "called in sick" or made excuses to someone else's job or school?
4. Have you ever not called the police after the person became physically abusive?
5. Have you ever let a person live with you because he or she has run out of money?
6. Has this person repeatedly run out of money, and you continually loan him or her money to cover his or her needs?
7. Have you ever bailed someone out of jail for an arrest connected with drugs or alcohol and/or physical abuse?
8. Have you ever excused someone from keeping a commitment because he or she is "depressed?"
9. Are you afraid to confront someone about his or her behaviors because you are afraid of violence?
10. Are you afraid to confront someone about his or her behaviors because you are afraid he or she will leave you?
11. Do you sometimes believe a person's behaviors are not so bad because "the problems are only occurring at home?"
12. Do you sometimes act as if you believe the person's excuses even when you know he or she is lying?

13. Do you sometimes think that it is your fault that someone behaved a particular way?
14. Do you prefer not to talk to anyone about the problem because you're ashamed?
15. Do you allow the person to come back to the house even after he or she has been physically destructive?
16. Do you make excuses to others for the person's behaviors?
17. Do you threaten negative consequences for someone's bad behavior, and then not follow through?
18. Do you pretend a chemically dependent person is sick when he or she is really coming off of a binge?
19. Have you ever taken drugs or drunk alcohol with the chemically dependent person so you can be together?
20. Have you ever obtained drugs or alcohol for a chemically dependent person?

If you have answered "yes" to three or more of these questions, consider the possibility that your help may actually be enabling. That means you are helping your son or daughter in the short term, but it might be hurting them in the long term. Fortunately, enabling is something you will learn to overcome as you become more educated about healthy helping.

Codependency Is Not Healthy Dependency

Under the age of eighteen, children are not their own official and actual authority. Parents are responsible for their children legally and morally and have absolute power and control over them. Children are also dependent upon their parents for food, shelter, clothing, emotional support, and educational and moral development. When they become adults, however, we can lapse into **codependency**.

There are several definitions of codependency commonly used today. Some clinicians call codependency "rationalized selfishness." Others actually consider it a disease, so the term "the disease to please" is often heard in treatment center halls.

Codependency is quite a complex subject, but can be seen simply as over-helping others to the detriment of yourself. It might also be defined as one adult helping another adult, but acting like a parent helping a child.

In extreme cases, it can be *pathological*. Here the codependent has unresolved issues they are avoiding dealing with. This type of avoidance is not unlike the workaholic who is using work as his focus to avoid facing the pain of resolving his own emotional issues.

If we look at the beginning of human development, we see that babies are naturally dependent on their mothers. The baby obviously cannot survive physically or emotionally without the mother's help. So the baby's dependency on the mother is quite obvious.

The way mothers are dependent on their children may not be as obvious. When you think of a mother being dependent upon her baby, what comes to mind? She certainly does not need the child for her physical well-being, so it must be for her emotional well-being. If traditionally, the father's job is to feed and protect his family, then the mother's traditional job can be described as keeping the home and raising the children. As a mom with a 22 year old alcoholic son once told me:

"Caring for my children's needs has pretty much been my life's work."

How much attachment does a mother have to her job of raising the children? Would she be suicidal if she were suddenly fired? Would she be disappointed, hurt, and sad when her children grew up and did not need her to raise them anymore? These are some of the normal and natural emotional issues all mothers face in their family and household careers.

So what happens if a mother who is normally dependent on being the nurturer to her babies carries that intense emotion and dependency forward into the time when her children became adults? And what about fathers? They are traditionally not as emotionally intensive as mothers, but they, too, may not realize that their interaction with their children should change when those offspring become adults.

It is these parental roles that are the foundational and natural underpinnings from which the problem of codependency is formed. So you might say that, if you are an adult who is overly dependent on another adult, you are codependent.

With this general description of codependency, we realize that codependency is a very common form of relationship in our culture today. Couples and friends are sometimes codependent, too.

There are many books written on the subject if you wish to delve deeper into it, but for our purposes, we will focus on the problem of codependency defined as, "a parent treating an adult son or daughter as if he or she were still a child" who, in fact, was dependent on the parent.

As previously noted, this dependency legally ends at age eighteen for the child. Nonetheless, this unhealthy dependence of grown children on their parents or parents on their children can create real problems, especially when addiction is in the picture.

Providing More Precise Help
One of the major challenges for many people is understanding that healthy helping is **precise helping** (help in very specific situations and ways) and most often is *much less help* than you would provide someone who doesn't have an addiction problem.

Most parents do not need to learn how to help their son or daughter more. They need to learn how to help their sons or daughters *less* ... and know that it helps them more.

This "less is more" strategy goes against most of our usual thinking. You might assume, "The more I care about you, the more help I should give." How could less help ever be good?

For instance, if your son or daughter has an addiction problem, the reality is that, most often, he or she must be in desperate straits before having sufficient motivation to ask for help to change his or her way of living.

So helping your loved one by providing, for instance, rent money while he or she is using other funds to buy drugs or alcohol isn't really helping.

Because most parents tend to over-help an addicted son or daughter, precise help most often seems to be providing less help. This is where the concept of **enabling** comes from. The theory is that, by providing more financial help than you need to, you are enabling your son or daughter to continue to buy and use drugs or alcohol. This is not your intention, but it can be the result.

Precise help is not over-helping or under-helping. Providing precise help to your adult child is not easy, especially in a society where the distinction between adult and child is so blurred, but through time and effort it can be learned.

One of the most important points to remember is to *treat your adult child like an adult even if he or she is not acting like an adult.*

It does not come naturally to provide less help to someone in need. But this approach can be learned, and a parent's willingness to put in the time and effort to learn how to provide more precise help to an addicted son or daughter can be considered a profound act of love.

Through time, and because of your efforts, you will have a new level of awareness. Along with practicing new habits of talking to and interacting with your adult child, helping less will, in essence, be a sort of rite of passage into adulthood.

How do you know when and how to help? The Two Cardinal Rules for Helping can clarify this for you.

Cardinal Rules for Helping
It's important to make a distinction between your loved one's asking for help to get well versus asking for help with day-to-day living. This can be confusing.

It's helpful, especially as you are learning these new habits, to stop for a moment and, before you help your addicted adult child, ask whether the help he or she is requesting will contribute to him or her getting well or whether it is just helping your loved one get through another day on drugs or alcohol.

For example, Bart's mom called me to ask the best way to help her twenty-six-year-old son who had no stable place to live, was still using meth, and was asking for money for food. She asked whether it would be all right to buy him a gift card from a grocery store so that she knew the money would go for groceries instead of drugs.

"Is it possible for a person to stand outside a grocery store and sell a gift card at a discount for cash?" I asked her.

She replied, "I've never heard of that before, but knowing my son, not only is it possible, it's likely."

So that's a good example of how virtually any financial help for daily expenses can be diverted.

Helping him or her get through another day of addiction is not necessarily helping. This is the first thing you need to determine: whether this is help you want to give at all. You can see the importance of your new learning to help you increase the likelihood that all of your decisions will be good ones.

Once you know that, there are two rules that will be quite helpful when your son or daughter is asking outright for assistance or implying he or she could use some. This is an important part of treating your loved one as the adult he or she is.

Cardinal Rule #1: "Give No Un-Asked-For Help"
Do not volunteer help.

Remember, you are reinforcing the fact that your loved one is an adult, and an adult should be mature enough to understand his or her own situation and know what is needed to address it.

Although there are times when we are able to recognize someone else's situation when they are too stressed to see it, you need to practice this rule consistently to communicate to your addicted adult child that he or she is, in fact, an adult and needs to use his or her coping skills.

Quite often, parents will say, "But he doesn't ask for help!" Their adult children will hint. He or she will talk about being worried about covering bills, for example, but not come right out and say, "I need help."

That's because *he or she doesn't have to ask for help*. He or she has you trained to think for him or her and offer help that he or she hasn't even asked for.

Your addicted loved one has no responsibility at all. So if the help works out, he or she gains no self-esteem because the action wasn't his or her decision. It was yours.

If it doesn't work out, he or she also doesn't get the benefit of the lesson that results in self-esteem as, again, the decision was yours.

In other words, your addicted adult child learns nothing about how to handle responsibility as an adult.

This sounds easy until that first call comes. What do you do when he or she calls you and says, "I'm hungry"?

Your response is simple:

"Oh."   Or "Bummer."

Or "That sucks."

And then *you shut up*.

Do your best to keep your tone calm and noncommittal.

Make your loved one ask for what he or she wants. Like an adult.

Consciously or unconsciously, he or she knows this game well. Addicts first danced this dance a long time ago, usually beginning early in childhood. Many addicts have gotten used to avoiding responsibility and are quite pleased to have their parents jump in and help them avoid it.

It is so blissfully easy *not* to have to be responsible! Someone else makes the decision, someone else is wrong if things don't go well. Successes are never achieved though. The sad fact remains that many do not mind the resulting loss of self-esteem that comes from this exchange; often because they have never experienced self-esteem and do not fully realize its value.

As an adult, however, both the challenges and rewards of accepting responsibility are yours.

Taking responsibility, even in the smallest areas, is an adult coping skill. This is something children will often avoid, especially when they are not willing to grow or change.

So as we see this game more clearly and refuse to play it any longer, change begins to take place, change we have been wanting to see for perhaps a long time.

This is the sort of change that is often small and incremental; **baby steps**, not dramatic and instant. It often takes a lot of small shifts to add up to a powerful change.

So when you hear the complaint but do not hear your addicted adult child ask for what he or she wants, when you're patient and do not take the bait, who knows what he or she will say?

If you are persistent and consistent, your loved one will eventually make the commitment of asking for what he or she wants.

You don't need to work your way up to this approach. Your adult child can be expected to ask for help like the adult he or she already is. He or she needs to start sometime, and that time can't be too soon.

It may take some practice on your part to learn this new habit. You might practice with your counselor, a friend, your mate, or even in the mirror. If you are not perfect at it at first, just keep applying your new knowledge. Practicing it makes you more comfortable with the new role you are developing and ready to handle the requests that your son or daughter are likely to make. You will continue to improve at it, and so will your adult child.

If, as you wait for your son or daughter to ask for what he or she wants, you get a partial commitment; for instance, "I need money". That's better, but not good enough. You want an adult response.

At this point, you might ask, "How much?" He or she might continue the dance by responding, "I don't know!" Your answer can be, "Well, let me know when you do know."

Your goal is to force your adult child to be specific about what help he or she is asking for. Your loved one needs to face up to reality and take responsibility for it. Making him or her articulate their desire is part of accepting responsibility for his or her own situation.

After you have waited patiently, your loved one may ask for example, $200. Now you are now ready to employ Cardinal Rule #2.

Cardinal Rule #2: "No Instant Answer"

That's right, we're making your son or daughter wait on purpose. Usually, when he or she wants money or some other form of help, it's a crisis. Whether or not this technique is intentional, the result is that he or she can squeeze a "yes" out of you more quickly. Even though you may regret it later, it's hard to say "no" when you feel pressure so creatively applied.

No instant answer means, simply, no instant answer. So when you are asked for the $200, for instance, you answer simply, "I'll get back to you on that."

Now you might run into more pressure. "But I need to know right now! They're going to kick me out of here if I don't come up with the money now!"

This reason might actually be true, but it took a long time to get to this place. For example, if he or she is requesting money for rent, how long do you think your loved one has owed the money? How many times has he or she been asked for it before it gets to this place?

Fortunately, you are prepared to respond to that pressure. Simply reply, "I need to talk to someone else first, and I will get back with you. If you need to know right this moment, then the answer is no."

In other words, if an instant answer is insisted upon, and it is not literally a life-and-death issue in that moment, the pressure for an instant answer generates an automatic "no".

The conflict for you as a "good parent" is that your job description includes making sure your child never gets to the end of his or her rope. But your child is now an adult, and he or she must be in charge of his or her own life.

Always providing an instant answer can prevent an addict from being motivated to seek help.

How? By preventing the addict from having to face the consequences of his or her destructive actions.

> "No consequences, no new learning.
> No new learning, no change."

I am often asked by parents, "Why does he or she continue to do this despite the consequences?"

Often I respond, "What consequences?" Or I will point out that he or she continues to act this way because he or she can. *You might be unintentionally helping him or her continue this predictable cycle of avoiding change.*

The 'Big Five' Ways to Show Love

We've talked about enabling, codependency, helping, and guilt. So how do you show your love to your adult child?

You *do* love your addicted son or daughter, but how do you react when you don't give into his or her requests and then hear, "I guess you don't really love me," or some version of that?

For instance, if your adult child is asking for money that you suspect might be used for drugs or alcohol, and you refuse to give the money, your loved one very well might say, "I thought you loved me." How can you respond to this statement?

One effective response is, "Pack your bags — we're taking a guilt trip." By saying this, you are "calling" him or her on the emotional blackmail being used. In fact, by making him or her face up to his or her own responsibility, you are truly showing your love.

Nonetheless, he or she might persist in accusing you of not loving him or her. This is a time for either silence, or for explaining that it is because you love him or her that you are insisting that your loved one takes responsibility for his or her actions.

It also can be helpful to remind yourself that giving money or other forms of financial support to your adult child is not the only way to show love.

Here are five ways to show love that do not include financial support.

We call them the Big Five Ways to Show Love:

1. Words of encouragement

These words can be communicated as "I love you." "I believe in you." "I know you'll beat this problem." etc.

56

People generally hear disapproval twice as loud as they hear approval, so you need to redouble your efforts to show your love to your son or daughter.

2. Letters

Letters are written words of encouragement. They may seem old-fashioned, but because they are seldom written these days, they often mean even more to their recipients. Your letter may be something you leave in your loved one's room if he or she is living with you, something you mail to wherever he or she is living, or in the case where you don't know where your adult child is, something you write and keep for him or her. Depending on the situation, many parents have opted to send letters instead of personal visits when their loved one is incarcerated.

3. Hugs

Hugs provide a physical interaction that is irreplaceable. Hugging isn't something that just happens between parents and children under eighteen. It is a worldwide indication of affection, and adults hug all the time.

4. Prayers

Prayer is optional, but many people find it helpful. It is something you can do whether or not you are in contact with your loved one. At the very least, the prayers will make you feel better, but there is always the hope that your adult child will benefit from the prayers or even simply from knowing you are praying for him or her.

5. Sharing a meal

You can share a meal together in your home if there is enough trust left or built, but this is a tricky situation. I work with many parents who feel an obligation to bring their adult child home for a meal even when they've experienced theft in their home or other negative interactions, such as violence. In these cases, it's highly recommended that you meet in a restaurant.

When necessary, you can always say to your addicted adult child, "I will always love you, and I will always give you words of encouragement when I talk to you, write letters to you when you're not around, give you hugs when you are around, pray for you, and take you out to a meal. Now tell me those are not ways to show love."

Of course, you must follow through on these actions. Keep these opportunities to show your love in mind to balance out the new limits, boundaries, and consequences you are learning to put into practice with your son or daughter.

Childish vs. Childlike
The Challenges of Delayed Emotional Growth

A short definition of **Delayed Emotional Growth**: "A dysfunctional condition experienced by a child who has matured physically and intellectually but not psychologically and has difficulty coping with the normal stresses and responsibilities of adulthood."

As we have discussed, unlike adults, children are not the authority of their own lives. If little Johnny wants food, he gets it from his parents. Yes, Johnny can get food from others and borrow money from friends or relatives, but the bottom line is that all of his survival needs are, according to our social and cultural norms, met by his parents.

A child does not have the power of choice in major life decisions; his parents do. Having choice is the very definition of empowerment. So all children, by definition, are naturally **disempowered** until they become adults at age eighteen.

All of a sudden at age eighteen, Johnny now has the power of absolute choice over and responsibility for himself. How does life look now? How does life feel now? This is such a dramatic shift in Johnny's world, yet how much time does he get to adjust to this new "gift"; how much time to learn how to use this new power of choice? Also, how much time does Johnny's parents have to adjust to this life-changing event?

He is legally his own authority now and can own property, join the service, get married, and vote. Now he also must get his own needs met by himself. Does he have the necessary **adult coping skills** to be successful in this great adventure called adulthood?

Often, nobody knows the answer to this question. Unlike some Native American and other indigenous cultures and religions such as Judaism and Catholicism, our American society has no rite of passage that formalizes the transition from child to adult. One day you are a seventeen-years-and-three-hundred-and-sixty-four-day-old child and the next day you are an adult.

Even the obvious rite of graduating from high school at eighteen is now blurred because so many children are expected to go to college, which their parents pay for.

Without a structured **rite of passage**, there are no guidelines to look at and measure. What are the critical skills necessary for a person to get his or her needs met as an adult? And how do we teach these life skills?

This topic deserves further discussion at another time, but it is critical to understanding the child–parent dynamic to acknowledge how many people never realize the responsibility for their behavior and actions because they unintentionally were never prepared for adulthood.

When children fail to make the transition from childhood to adulthood, they suffer from delayed emotional growth, a condition that often results in codependency and childishness even in those who are legally adults.

We live in a culture that pretends that, when you reach age eighteen, you're somehow magically given adult coping skills. Unfortunately, for any number of reasons, many adults never really grew up, and thus their emotional growth remains as stunted as if they were a child. They, however, are not.

Fortunately, emotional growth can occur even in our adult years. But, for addicts, they must be in recovery from their addiction before emotional growth can take place.

It also doesn't help that our society has never developed an agreed-upon list of adult coping skills. If we had such a list, we could make sure, as a society, that these adult coping skills would be taught to our children prior to reaching their age of maturity.

In your own life, you may have learned some adult coping skills without really knowing what they were. As a child of previous generations, there was more opportunity for "instructional" experiences with a wide range of adults. Most of us learned a healthy decision-making strategy, for example, but we can't say how we learned it. Perhaps you had more options for such **teachable moments** because you had more time to interact with a neighbor, grocer, barber, or teacher as well as your parents.

Previously, a whole village had unspoken permission to impart such knowledge through interactions with children. Back then, there were more adult teachers available to instruct children who, for instance, were caught stealing. A shopkeeper might threaten or even paddle a young boy back then, or call his parents.

The benefits of an adult lesson being imparted informally was obvious. Such an incident was not just a lesson in morals, it was also an opportunity for a child to learn about good decision making by experiencing the painful consequences of making a bad decision. From such experiences, the wisdom of thinking through decisions can be practiced and learned.

In his book *The Social Animal* (Random House, 2011), social commentator and author David Brooks acknowledges the problem:

> Modern society has created a giant apparatus for the cultivation of the hard skills, while failing to develop the moral and emotional faculties down below. Children are coached on how to jump through a thousand scholastic hoops. Yet by far the most important decisions they will make are about whom to marry, whom to befriend, what to love and what to despise, and how to control impulses. On these matters they are almost entirely on their own. We are good at talking about material incentives, but bad about talking about emotions and intuitions. We are good at teaching technical skills, but when it comes to the most important things, like character, we have almost nothing to say.

For example, healthy decision making, the ability to weigh factors and come to a decision, is an adult coping skill. Children do not necessarily need that skill as long as they remain a child (age seventeen or younger) because their parents are responsible for their decisions. Adults, however, definitely need to hone this skill as they will use it often.

Think about how you learned healthy decision making. Most often, people will say they are not certain but suspect they learned it from some person or experience in the past. In many cases, the people involved in the lesson weren't aware of the importance of what they had taught. This is the essence of an informal rite of passage. It's there, but we can't define it. That's why, over the past fifty years, we didn't notice our gradual loss of the value of such interactions in our society.

As a parent, if you can't be sure how you learned your decision-making strategy, *how could you teach it*? Even if you are absolutely certain about how you learned to make healthy decisions, you likely won't be able to explain exactly how to make them. Again, how could you be expected to teach it?

If you have an addicted adult child who is lying, manipulating, making poor decisions, displaying excessive anger, not taking responsibility for his or her actions, and is unable to delay gratification, we could make the argument your adult child is still using a young child's coping skills.

Now, however, is now. We must live in the present and learn new ways to teach our children adult coping skills. When we are faced with adult children who lack them, we must reinforce the importance of adult actions, which is just what you are now learning to do.

Remember our discussion about false guilt versus true guilt? This is another time when you can remind yourself that it can be very helpful for both you and your adult child to forgive yourselves for something you could not have known. We discussed the importance of only feeling guilty when you knowingly do something wrong. This is a good time for you to remember once again that false guilt comes from feeling guilty about something you did wrong, but at the time did not know was wrong.

This is one of the pitfalls of being a human being. You can use knowledge you just gained as a stick to beat yourself with as you look back at a situation in which you did the best you could with what you knew then. Or you can look back at such a situation and pretend you knew back then what you actually didn't, and then feel guilty.

Once you get over the normal guilt and often shame that all parents feel about not being perfect parents, you can spend more of your mental energy learning new skills. Chief among them might be treating your adult son or daughter more like an adult.

This is, admittedly, difficult when he or she is acting like a youth: acting up, acting out, lying, manipulating, not taking responsibility for decisions, etc. Without an approved list of adult coping skills, we are subject to a **cultural blind spot** that is responsible for many of our problems today.

While delayed emotional growth is a separate issue, when it's coupled with substance abuse, these two problems fuel one another. If we don't identify and address the delayed emotional growth problem, we limit our ability to help the addict or alcoholic achieve a successful, long-term recovery.

It's important to note delayed emotional growth does not just go away with age. As long as an addict avoids recovery, they are avoiding their emotional growth. The oldest addict I've counseled admitted having all of the traits listed on the next page. He was 74 years old.

Being childish is not the same as being childlike. In general, we say people are childlike when they possess such qualities as being playful, open-minded, excited about learning, etc. In general, we might think of people who are childish as petty, attention-demanding, self-centered, irresponsible, unreliable, etc.

Below is a list of childish traits associated with alcoholics and addicts who have not achieved adult maturity and continue to demonstrate a consistent immaturity and self-centeredness in their behaviors.

Delayed Emotional Growth Traits:

- Lies.

- Steals.

- Breaks promises.

- Resents authority.

- Wants instant gratification.

- Takes "no" too personally.

- Excessively controlling.

- Excessively angry (but it's not always obvious).

- Makes poor decisions.

- Refuses to accept full responsibility for his or her own decisions.

- Excessively selfish at times and excessively unselfish at other times.

- Lacks boundaries.

Dishonesty is not just a moral problem, it is also a **child's coping skill**. Because children are not their own authority, they must manipulate the authorities who control their lives to get their needs met. Not being their own authority, they are not responsible for their decisions. Whoever is in authority over them is responsible for them.

Dishonesty is not a child's only coping skill. It is just one characteristic of delayed emotional growth that is actually a natural and normal coping skill for children. Other coping skills include impatience, excessive reactive anger, and poor decision making.

When your adult son or daughter has these sorts of childish coping skills and lacks adult coping skills, it seems like he or she has never really "left home" emotionally. Your adult child may be afraid to live in a sober "not-so-easy-to-manipulate" environment. Often there will always be a parent, spouse, relative, or friend available to rescue him or her from painful consequences of life.

Accordingly, your adult child may feel incapable of living a successful adult life without being able to use drugs or alcohol to cope.

The Three D's
Because of their fear of moving forward in their own lives, addicts are often skilled at avoiding their own problems by focusing everyone on something else.

They can do this by employing what we call the **Three D's**:
- *Delay*

    Johnny never finds the time to do his homework or pay back a loan.

- *Distract*

    Johnny might tell his parents what problems they need to work on in *their* life; to distract from his his own.

- *Deny*

    Johnny says, "My drug use isn't that big of a problem — everybody does it."

The Three D's are actually conscious or unconscious coping mechanisms that children learn in childhood to avoid doing things they are afraid of or don't really want to do. These are the same tools children use to stay safe in situations they cannot understand and certainly have no control over.

See if you can identify some of these childish characteristics in this recent story, paraphrased from a newspaper:

17–Month Term for Hollywood Bad Boy

A 42-year-old Hollywood actor was sentenced today to two years in jail and six months in a drug-treatment facility for repeatedly failing drug tests while free on probation. He remains free while appealing an assault conviction. He pleaded with the judge for leniency, saying he had broken his parents' hearts and felt like a fifteen-year-old boy. The actor told the judge, "I'm not acting this time." He begged for leniency, saying he couldn't imagine a future without performing. Outside the court, he gave a high-five and directed his middle finger at the press.

Can you recognize the delayed emotional growth traits in this story? They're a lot more obvious when you are educated about them.

Suffering from both addiction and delayed emotional growth at the same time can lead a person to feel hopeless. They may feel, "I'll never be able to change." That's because *addiction and delayed emotional growth both cause resistance to change*. This is true because they reinforce each other.

And although addiction can eventually be diagnosed, delayed emotional growth is often impossible to identify through our cultural eyes.

The most common cause of delayed emotional growth is the abuse of alcohol or drugs during a person's early twenties or younger. It's important to note that such abuse of alcohol or drugs as a child is not the only cause. It can be a major contributing reason, but there are many other factors, such as genetics, temperament, chance, abuse and even the perception of abuse that contribute to the creation of this problem.

The most important thing we need to keep in mind is that, no matter what the cause or causes, we have no clear way to know when a person needs extra help in learning adult coping skills. As we have noted, we don't even have a simple list of what those skills are!

Without agreed-upon skills that children need to be successful as adults in our society, how can we be sure our children have them before we send them off into adulthood? How can we successfully solve this issue?

Having a poorly defined problem, severely limits your ability to solve it. One of the positive side effects of addiction and recovery is that they can provide the opportunity to see this invisible issue of delayed emotional growth. We can now identify and describe the problem, and most important, we can finally solve it.

The positive side of knowing that your addicted child is simply using the only coping skills he or she knows, means he or she can still learn the adult coping skills necessary to replace them.

Adult coping skills such as honesty, healthy decision making, patience, anger management, taking responsibility for decisions, etc. can be taught and learned. Fortunately, recovery from addiction to drugs and alcohol is a process that, through time, teaches such skills. It teaches them indirectly, yet it teaches them in a powerful way.

Where else might a person learn such skills? There are other places where these skills are taught to some degree. For instance going into military service, going to jail, going to prison, joining a gang. Like going into recovery from drugs and alcohol abuse, these can be looked upon as default rites of passage.

Without an agreed-upon list of adult coping skills, parents are not responsible for this delayed emotional growth phenomenon and neither are their children. Our society, which seems to be asleep when it comes to this issue, is ultimately responsible. From this viewpoint, then all of us in this society, in our own way, are responsible for having an unacknowledged problem.

There isn't an official list of adult coping skills, so let us at least acknowledge the ones we know.

Here is a proposed list that counters the list of the delayed emotional growth characteristics/child coping skills we shared earlier:

Adult Coping Skills:
- Being honest
- Earning your own money legally
- Keeping commitments, or re-negotiating when necessary
- Submitting to authority when it's beneficial to do so
- Delaying gratification (being patient), when necessary
- Accepting the answer "no" without taking it personally
- Giving up control when it's best to do so
- Managing anger
- Making responsible decisions, recognizing the good ones and learning from the bad ones
- Accepting responsibility for all of your decisions
- Limiting selfishness (setting and keeping boundaries with self)
- Limiting unselfishness (setting and keeping boundaries with others)

While this may not be a complete list of adult coping skills, it is at least one upon which most people can all agree. One we can perhaps refine and add to as our understanding of this complex and confusing issue grows.

When children learn these adult coping skills, they can finally leave home, both physically and emotionally. Then they can become an independent and responsible adult who enjoys living a sober life. They will also be able to refuse **unhealthy rescuing** (situations in which they are offered the opportunity to be enabled).

Jackson's Story

Jackson, an eighteen-year-old who lived at home with his parents and two sisters, had just graduated from high school, but he had been using heroin and opiate prescription pills for approximately two years. He'd been able to hide his addiction to these drugs for about a year-and-a-half.

When his parents found out and confronted him, he lied to them about his drug use. When they had him tested, however, they realized he really did have an addiction. After attending a couple of PAL meetings, Jackson's parents called me for a family session.

We first scheduled a family education coaching session. Jackson was told that we were going to conduct a family session of brainstorming options and choices he could make to move forward in his life.

He was open to attending, and we talked about the issues around addiction. He did not admit to being an addict but did say that he had a problem with drugs and could not control his usage. Jackson also admitted to many of the symptoms or problems of delayed emotional growth such as dishonesty, unwillingness to take responsibility for his decisions, poor decision making, the inability to delay gratification and to practice patience, and excessive anger issues.

During the session, Jackson listened to some of the feedback from his parents and his sisters and said he would enter treatment. He completed a thirty-day rehab inpatient program and then participated in an intensive outpatient program. During the two months of intensive outpatient treatment, Jackson lived in a sober living home with other recovering addicts. At present, he is living at home and doing well.

Jackson's story is not typical, but it is worth knowing that good things can happen in situations that seem hopeless.

It is much more commonplace to have more drama and situations occur before a person is willing to enter treatment, but sometimes addicts are ready to change their lives when they are truly faced with their problems.

Drug Addict or Drug Abuser?
As the parent of an addict or alcoholic, your education can help you realize that your adult child may not be an addict. There are sometimes complications and confusion over this diagnosis. It may take some time to discover the truth. "Is he or she addicted or just abusing drugs [or alcohol]?" The further complication is that all signs may point to addiction, but he or she may not, however, be quite ready to accept it.

I like the saying:
Addiction is the only disease that needs to be self-diagnosed.

In other cases, people may realize and accept that they are addicts as young teens because of personal experiences.

But there can be a battle over *reality*. Whatever his or her perception, it's important to not label your son or daughter, because it just becomes an unwinnable battle that can sidetrack you from the battles that can be won.

I am a strong proponent of asking your loved one, "Do you consider yourself an alcoholic or addict?"

The next important step is to *really listen and accept the other person's reality even if we don't agree with it*. Arguing will get you nowhere, but understanding his or her perception helps you know what you are dealing with.

We can then help lead our loved one to the truth from where he or she is rather than where we think he or she should be.

Yes, your loved one may be in denial. The question is whether a frontal attack will work better than a cooperative approach.

That being said, paradoxically, there *are* times when we need to force our loved ones to get help. This is an example of what makes knowing the right thing to do so difficult. In this situation, going to a reliable treatment center and getting an evaluation from a professional can help, as can talking to an **interventionist**.

My main point is for you as the parent to get out of the theoretical argument with your adult child about whether he or she is an addict and move on to the discussion about getting help either way.

For instance, as one father put it when talking to his son who was abusing cocaine and had lost everything, "I'm not arguing with you, son, over whether you are an addict or not. The reality is, cocaine has been a problem for you, and treatment will help you either way."

You cannot lead a person from where they are not. So when I ask, "Do you consider yourself to be an addict?" and hear, "No, I don't think I am an addict," I can then ask the question, "Have drugs [or alcohol] been a problem for you in your life?"

In my twenty-five years of counseling, I have never worked with anyone who had a drug or alcohol problem answer "No".

Interestingly enough, most often when I ask the question about whether the person thinks he or she is an addict, the person I am asking replies "Yes". I can then use the term without inviting resistance because that person has accepted it for him or herself.

As you might have already guessed, I recommend to parents that they do not label their adult child as an addict or alcoholic, but rather suggest they use the same term that their son or daughter uses to self-label.

If that person is not an addict or alcoholic by his or her own definition, we can say, "What do you think you need to do for your drug or alcohol problem?" *Whatever answer is given is the beginning of our planning for your loved one moving forward and getting some help.*

We are now operating from common ground: his or her perceived state.

In speaking with someone who has a drug or alcohol problem, I can realistically argue that even if you are not an alcoholic or addict, you can still benefit from addiction counseling and/or outpatient treatment. That's because such counseling and treatment teaches life skills (adult coping skills) not just **abstinence** from drugs and alcohol.

Anyone who can benefit from learning some of these coping skills (and that's pretty much all of us) can have a better life by attending such counseling or treatment.

Some people will try "putting on the hat" of being an alcoholic or addict and attend twelve-step meetings such as Alcoholics Anonymous, Narcotics Anonymous, Pills Anonymous, Cocaine Anonymous, etc.

to discover more personal truth. Whether your adult child admits to be an addict or alcoholic or only admits to having a problem with drugs or alcohol, help is still available.

How Old Are You?

There is no word in the English language to differentiate between a child and an adult child. Think about all of the common synonyms for the word "child": "baby", "innocent", "kid", "lamb", "little angel", "little darling", "little doll", "little one", "adolescent", "youngster", "boy", and "girl". Do you use one of these words to describe an adult son or daughter?

Now let's look at the synonyms for "adult": "developed", "grown", "grownup", "man", "woman".

There are reasons why parents carry around an old *picture* in their minds as the reality for their adult child. They are not stupid; they are merely in error. A mom might *see* her twenty-five-year-old son as a twelve-year-old because he is acting like a twelve-year-old. This is easy for her to do since she knew him when he was a twelve-year-old.

Your perception is your reality, and if you perceive your adult child as age seventeen or younger, your reality is that you feel legally and morally responsible for him or her. There may be many reasons why you hold on to a mistaken reality, but regardless, you and your adult child will both suffer because of it.

Being aware of the mind-picture you carry of your adult child and the words you think of to describe him or her, helps you confirm the theory that you may be enabling your offspring. This may be because you believe you have no other choice.

Treating your addicted loved one as younger than eighteen is really disempowering for both you and your loved one. But, since it works for your loved one to get what he or she wants, he or she may well continue to take advantage of it, consciously or unconsciously.

For instance, you have no choice other than to get an adolescent child out of jail. But for an adult, jail may be the best experience at a particular time. Until now, this distinction may have been unconscious, but now, through education, it is coming to the surface for you.

No matter what the reason, though, the outcome is the same: parents who treat their adult loved one as a minor may be helping in the short term, but doing tremendous damage in the long-term.

The solution is simple but not easy. The answer is to become aware of the error of your thinking and correct it.

After all, you have practiced this habit of seeing your offspring as a youngster for a long time, and you will need to develop new habits to see him or her as an adult.

Many parents have told me they work hard at practicing over and over the task of changing their old and false picture of their son or daughter as an underage child to the new and true picture of his or her actual age. As Albert Einstein said, "Repetition is the mother of all new learning."

If you picture your son or daughter as underage and he or she has no addiction, it's not such a big deal. But when there also are addiction issues, along with delayed emotional growth, this combination can actually help maintain a sense of hopelessness.

Once again, there is no one to blame for this societal problem, which some would call a tragedy. We need to focus on solving the problem instead of blaming anyone. It may take parents a bit of time and practice to change the picture in their minds of their sons or daughters, but it is tremendously important that they do. Fortunately, the more you practice, the better you get at it.

In our PAL groups, we ask first-time visitors, "How old is your substance-abusing son or daughter in your mind?" It is striking how often the answer is, "Well, he acts like a twelve-year-old" or a similar age. Many parents say the picture they are holding onto in their minds reflects a time before drug use, when their child was innocent.

This is really important, because the picture in your mind is your reality and the basis of your decision making. You can see how many problems can occur because you are making decisions for, say a twenty-year-old, as if he or she were a twelve-year-old.

After coming to meetings for perhaps a month or so, parents sometimes report that they are now seeing their twenty-something aged children as age eighteen. This is progress from the image they used to hold of, for instance, a fourteen-year-old.

When you **empower** your adult child, you also expect him or her to accept the responsibilities of being an adult. Simply put, the definition of empowerment is having more choices. Therefore being disempowered means you have fewer choices or no choices at all. So another way of looking at this type of education is that it's empowering you, in your role as a parent, by giving you choices beyond what you could have known.

You can also learn to **pick your battles**, set boundaries and consequences. These things our culture does not do a good job of teaching us to do. As we've discussed, you'll also learn how to say less to the addicted person in your life. These and other adult interactions will serve both you and your adult child well.

Parent Roles

There are many parent roles that may need to be rewritten as you redefine your relationship with your adult child.

Here are some of the parental roles you may need to address:

1) **Enabler** — Has a strong need to take care of and please an addicted loved one.

2) **Codependent** — Has a strong need to take care of and please an addicted loved one, and everyone else.

3) **Rescuer** — Inadvertently keeps the addicted loved one in a dependent position.

4) **Enforcer** — Plays the part of "policeman" for the addicted loved one.

5) **Ignorer** — Gives up because "nothing works".

6) **Punisher** — Tries to use punishment to force the addicted loved one to change.

7) **Controller** — Tries to help the addicted loved one change by controlling all of his or her decisions.

8) **Jailer** — Tries to help the addicted loved one change by keeping him or her safe at home.

9) **Lecturer** — Tries to lecture, criticize, or give advice to get the addicted loved one to change.

10) **Pretender** — Acts like everything is OK while hoping things will somehow get better.

Through a Parent's Eyes

These are roles people slip into unconsciously while trying to help the addict in their lives. All can relate to treating someone as a child instead of an adult, and all are most often the wrong sort of helping.

When an adult child is still living at home with his or her parents, there can be an extra level of drama and frustration in the household because of his or her alcohol or drug use. Even though alcohol or drugs might be the root of the extra drama in your child's life, it is not always the obvious cause. One common *red flag* with this potentially hidden problem, is the lack of gratitude on the part of your adult child. This can be very frustrating for parents who have been going out of their way to help their son or daughter achieve a successful life.

A good example of this frustration occurred while I was helping a mom and dad with their nineteen-year-old son Larry, who was living with them, going to school, and working. This young man had a two-year problem with opiate prescription painkillers that started with a back injury that occurred at work. Because the drug use began legitimately, Larry did not consider himself to be an addict. He did admit to abusing prescription painkillers by using more than was prescribed.

After receiving a ticket for driving under the influence, losing his girlfriend, and having to go to the hospital because of an overdose, he finally admitted to having problems with drugs but not to being an addict.

During a session with his parents, I helped Larry formulate a written plan for eventually moving out of his childhood home into his own apartment. The plan required him to save a certain amount of money, but during the session, his parents told me how much they were helping him financially, including giving him a car to use so that he could go to work and even managing his money for him to the point of having him surrendering every paycheck to them.

They could not understand Larry's lack of gratitude, nor his rebellious attitude. In their eyes, Larry was acting like a spoiled brat, complaining about little things, and acting at times as if he was the man of the house in place of his father, something that did not go over very well.

While helping Larry formulate his plan, I had another goal in mind. I wanted Larry's parents to understand why Larry was acting this way. I told them that Larry was feeling like he could not be himself. Of course, they protested, insisting that they accepted Larry for what he was while bending over backwards to help him financially and emotionally. In fact, they felt they were helping him more than he actually deserved.

And they *were* helping him too much; they were over-helping. They were also continuing to treat Larry like a child, yet expecting him to act like an adult. This is a common problem between parents and children. Gradually, his parents began to understand that Larry was still formulating his identity and was overly sensitive to being told who he was instead of allowing him to be who he was. In short, he was feeling rejected by his parents, who were only trying to help him. You can see the dilemma here.

As I explained to his parents, if Larry had left home, over a period of months and years he might have gone through the process of becoming a man by facing and overcoming adversity and would not be so sensitive about this issue of identity. His parents were acting as if he had already gone through this process. Ironically, the more his parents over-helped Larry, doing things for him instead of letting him do them for himself, the more hostile Larry became.

Eventually Larry's parents were able to see that they were actually preventing him from the very experience of adversity that he needed so that he could become an adult. So his written plan also included ways for his parents to cut certain financial strings, which they were using to manipulate Larry to get him to do the "right" things.

Although Larry was pleased to have those strings cut so that he felt less manipulated and more able to make his own decisions, there was still a childish part of him that wanted to be taken care of and wanted a guarantee that no matter what he did, his parents would take care of him financially. Such is the ambivalence in the journey from childhood to adulthood.

Ultimately, Larry's parents felt some hope in their journey of helping him by cutting those financial strings, something we will discuss in more depth soon.

Even though many unknowns lay ahead for Larry and his family, his parents were becoming comfortable by deciding on a sensible path and trusting that they would learn whatever else they needed as they moved forward on this scary journey of change.

Their willingness to listen to suggestions and make changes became a model of hope and change for Larry. Now, his parents were doing what was suggested in their PAL Group: Changing their role from parenting a child to that of parenting an *adult* child. They were becoming role models for Larry instead of being his life coach.

They came to a moment when they could actually apologize to Larry for treating him like an underage child instead of the adult he was. They told me Larry said there was no need for the apology, but definitely seemed pleased to hear it.

This was a powerful moment for both of them and for Larry, one that allowed them all to move forward more decisively than before.

Magic Moment #3: Apologizing for Not Treating Your Adult Child Like an Adult.
"We love you very much, and thought we were helping by treating you like a child. Now we realize that you deserve to be treated like the adult you are."

It was also a time when Larry's parents could acknowledge that feeling guilty about their long-time mistaken treatment of their son would be false guilt. They did not realize what they were doing, so feeling guilty about their past behavior would not help them or Larry in any way.

This change in roles for parents is the formula to maximize their positive influence over an adult child who has an addiction problem.

The Strain on Marriages
Having an addicted adult child means having many problems. As a parent, you can become very easily overwhelmed with all that is going on. There is usually much drama and trauma, and it may seem to have no end. As parents try to help resolve the problems of a son or daughter addicted to drugs or alcohol and also struggle with the invisible issue of delayed emotional growth, their marriage can inevitably be stressed and strained.

There are many reasons for this strain. Chief among them is the entrenched habit of treating your son and daughter like a child, even though your loved one has reached the age of maturity. Often, one parent wants to treat their adult child as a grown-up and the other still sees him or her as an adolescent.

Another problem that will stress a marriage is the difference of opinion that can occur between a mother and father regarding decisions about how to help.

"Should we drug test?"

"Should we still pay for school?"

"What if our adult child steals from us — should we call the police?"

"What if our adult child lands in jail? Should we pay for an attorney? Should we bail our loved one out of jail as soon as possible?"

Parents who still see their children as younger than eighteen would understandably struggle with these sorts of issues. Seeing your loved one as an adult changes the answers considerably.

Perhaps the father, though, is seeing his adult child as eighteen or older. He no longer feels responsible for his addicted loved one, who is, after all, now an adult. He may even feel that his adult child needs this particular consequence to teach him or her a life lesson and doesn't see it as punishment. Meanwhile, the mom, the nurturer, may still see her adult child as her little baby.

So is it any wonder that a mother and father could get into an argument over what each of them feels is the best way to help? With different views on the adulthood of your child, you can see why it might be difficult if not impossible to come to a friendly agreement.

Another issue is gender. Men and women speak different languages, something that often goes unsaid but has been proven repeatedly in research such as that cited in books including Deborah Tannen's bestseller, *You Just Don't Understand.*

It isn't just language that's different. From working with literally hundreds of families, I truly believe that it takes a man to teach a boy to be a man, and a woman to teach a girl to be a woman. This is why programs such as Big Brothers and Big Sisters are so popular.

I also believe it's important for men and women to have the same gender counselor, sponsor, and healthy friends as well. A notable exception to this gender rule is the counselor assigned during

inpatient treatment. That's because this level of treatment is so foundational, the gender of a primary counselor is not as critical.

Unfortunately, as a young man reaches the age of eighteen, he usually no longer listens to his father and mother. If you doubt this, think back to your own years of growth and ask yourself when you stopped listening to your parents. Often, the people who get through to our adult children are not their parents but perhaps a counselor, sponsor, minister, or older friend. Having their children learn important life lessons from someone else can be painful for parents, but sometimes such education is more palatable coming from another person.

As parents begin this journey of learning to interact differently with their children, many of them can benefit from going to individual counseling separately as well as marriage counseling to deal with the stress and strain on their own relationship.

This is nothing to be ashamed of. In fact, quite the opposite. It is just another form of education.

In the long run, if the parents take care of their own marriage during this stressful time, their bond may be strengthened by the process. Having an addicted son or daughter can cause much strain on the parents' marriage. The upside is that the stress can reveal potential areas of improvements for the marriage.

Whatever the state of the relationship between them, it's important to note that parents who are trying their best to help their addicted son or daughter may not have the necessary education, or knowledge, to do so.

It's humbling to remind yourself that you were fired as your child's boss when he or she reached age eighteen. Recovery from addiction teaches not only abstinence from drugs and alcohol, it also indirectly helps develop a person's life skills, also known as adult coping skills. This is a silver lining in the dark cloud of addiction.

When There Are Multiple Parents
In our modern world in which divorce and remarriage is as common as couples staying together, people often have more than the traditional two parents. When step-parents are involved, helping an adult child can be even more complicated.

For instance, the mother of an addicted loved one who continues to educate herself and make positive changes to help her son or daughter, may have influence over her husband to some degree; even if he does not make much effort to educate himself. She may not, however, have any influence over an ex-husband or a stepmother.

Of course, the ideal situation is having all family members attend counseling, read the same books, and attend a support group that helps them adjust their perspectives and actions, but this does not always happen. In most cases, for whatever reason, more mothers attend meetings than fathers. But if Johnny has a mother, a father, a stepmother, and a stepfather, as many do, now he has four people to manipulate and to train to enable him. It's easy to see how this can complicate recovery.

In many situations, one parental couple has learned together and made some positive changes to help an addicted son or daughter, but how do you reach the other parents? Sometimes there is a good relationship between all four, but that is not always the case. Often, there is still some bitterness.

This unresolved history can play itself out in a form of unhealthy competition between the players. It may look something like, "Why aren't you helping Johnny? Why won't you let him live at home?

I'm going to let him live with me because I love him more than you do."

In July 2010, I visited with a divorced couple who had a heroin-addicted twenty-four-year-old daughter and each of the parents had new spouses. In the focused family educational session in my office, each parent could voice his or her opinions and concerns, and listen to each other's points of view. These moms and dads, after much spirited discussion, were able to come to some agreement about the best steps for helping their daughter. I think it was helpful for each parent to feel they were listened to and their opinion validated in the session.

This is an example of just one of many potential dramas that can play out between divorced parents. Consciously or unconsciously, you can bet an addicted son or daughter will manipulate any and all of these situations to his or her benefit.

Therefore, the ideal situation is for all parents to educate themselves and communicate with each other to have a **united front**. Agreement among these major players is absolutely essential to help an addicted adult child move forward.

It is often recommended that each couple go to counseling either individually or as a couple to resolve any of their past issues from previous marriages. Once again, it may not be obvious, but it is typical for the addicted son or daughter to use every bit of emotional leverage to continue to manipulate the most important people in his or her life.

That manipulation is how addicts attempt to take the focus off themselves, sometimes by playing parents against each other, to avoid having to change, grow up, and take personal responsibility.

Other family members are also involved and will have a variety of issues with the addict or alcoholic in their family. Brothers, sisters, uncles, aunts, cousins, for instance, typically do not have the amount of **leverage** and potential influence that parents and spouses possess.

It is very common for siblings of the alcoholic or addict to harbor resentment over being neglected by the same parents who are putting so much time, energy, and focus on the addicted child.

Other family members can also be victims of being lied to, taken advantage of, stolen from, etc. So all other family members of the addicted person will be affected in their own ways and could also benefit from going to counseling. With the help of a professional, family members can deal with the issues, the inevitable hurts, frustrations, and disappointments stemming from being in a relationship with an addict who is practicing his or her disease.

Janel's journey of helping her son Ernie is a great example of the risk and pain of change. It also demonstrates how she was able to take baby steps and gain the **incremental learning** she needed to help her son. Janel's story is one of her courage to change.

Janel Takes a Risk

By this time in Janel's journey, her son Ernie had been in and out of rehab several times for his opiate addiction, and even though he was twenty-six, he had never shown a consistent desire for recovery. Ernie had recently been asked to leave rehab for using heroin on the premises and was back living with a girlfriend who was also a drug addict. This was a major heartache for Janel as she continued to try to help him with his drug problem.

By the time Janel attended her first PAL meeting, she reported that Ernie was now living on the streets with a friend, and both of them were using heroin. She said she would often drive down to the area Ernie lived in, find him, and give him food. She also allowed Ernie to show up at her home at any time, come in, and take a shower. She was a loving mom and wanted to help her son.

As Janel began to learn the difference between enabling and healthy helping, she made some changes. After about two months of coming to PAL meetings, Janel reported that she called her son on his cell phone and told him that she would no longer be bringing food to him on the street. He responded, "Whatever."

She was obviously nervous about not feeding Ernie and worried about what would happen to him if she stopped her loving deliveries. Although this was never discussed, from an emotional standpoint, I believe Janel actually had to deal with the fear of her beloved son dying on the streets because she stopped bringing him food. As irrational as it sounds, I believe the powerful emotion of fear trumps logic every time.

About a month or so after Janel's announcement, she told the group that she had called Ernie and told him that he would not be allowed to come home and take showers anymore. Once again, she reported that Ernie said "Whatever" and hung up. Once again I believe Janel, a loving mother, had to grapple with that unreasonable fear about her son's survival.

After a couple more months of coming to meetings, Janel announced that she told Ernie that he needed to come and get the seven boxes of his personal items that had been stored in her garage for the past ten years. She offered to help him move the boxes and said she would give him thirty days' time to do so or would donate those boxes to Salvation Army. After about another month, she announced to the *group Ernie did not come and pick up his stuff and so she did indeed follow through with her commitment and donated the items to the Salvation Army.*

I believe Janel had to go through this terrible waiting period again to make sure that Ernie did not die. So, after another month or so, she announced to the group that she called her son and told him that she could not give him any more money for any reason. This time Ernie spouted an expletive and hung up on her.

Now another waiting period had to happen. Would Ernie die with no financial support from his mom? She assumed he would take odd jobs and daily labor to earn money and would panhandle to get money. She also suspected he may have been shoplifting and stealing in order to continue to live his sad, chosen lifestyle.

Janel may not have fully grasped the concept of cutting strings, but that is precisely what she had done. We will talk more about cutting strings later in this chapter. The important point is that by making those changes, in how she was helping her son, Janel was moving her son closer to being motivated to accept the help he needed to change.

Getting Out of Your Comfort Zone
Just like Janel, most parents who are trying to help their sons or daughters feel more comfortable doing what is known to them, which is what they have done before. This is part of human nature. Even if what they've done before doesn't work, continuing to do so somehow seems less uncomfortable than trying something new.

Most people are always more comfortable with the known than the unknown. This is an ever-present challenge any time life calls upon us to change what seems normal, no matter how miserable it may be.

Whatever our actions are, they seem normal to us because they have become habits we have practiced repeatedly. As habits, we do them without thinking.

But habit is a double-edged sword. Habits that are causing us problems are no less easy to change than habits that are helping us.

Take, for instance, the habit of *thinking for* your adult child when he or she is complaining about some circumstance of life. Johnny might say, "I've never been so depressed," or "I just don't know what to do. I've made such a mess of my life."

When you hear those type of complaints, do you offer help and advice? This is an example of how parents teach their young sons and daughters to face challenging and problematic situations in their lives. Your adult child, however, needs to be able to handle such issues without your help. What if someday you're not around to help?

This doesn't apply to adult children who occasionally do face especially difficult times, but rather those who live perpetually in a problem state because of their addictions.

For you to develop the new habits of not thinking for them, not giving them unsolicited advice or not giving them immediate help will take some doing, and it is something we will talk more about.

Juggling Challenges

Pinning your hopes on your adult child's progress only causes your level of hope to go up and down like a yo-yo. That's because your hope is based on situations outside of your control.

Now, instead of being in the disempowered position of having only one choice, you have now added the choice of measuring *your* progress as well. Two choices are real choice; one choice is no choice, and no choice is the essence of disempowerment. Now you can begin to feel hopeful because of the positive changes you are making. This is the essence of Spring.

So even if your adult child is not yet open to receiving help, you are able to move forward because *you* are receiving help.

When it comes to receiving help, you have a short-term goal and a long-term goal. Your short-term goal is to get professional help in making decisions. Your long-term goal is to learn how to make decisions yourself, which you do by committing to continue educating yourself about recovery from addiction.

Your **behavioral message** to your son or daughter is clear: "I love you enough to take the time to educate myself about your addiction, so I can best help you."

For most people, it is estimated to take about six months to a year to feel comfortable with your level of education. Regardless of how much time passes, however, you will have reached this accomplishment when you feel that

No matter what my son or daughter does,
I either know what to do,
or I know where to get the answer
to what is best to do.

You may even want to write this statement on a piece of paper and put it on your mirror or computer where you can see it and be reminded of it.

You will have reached this pinnacle by putting your new learning into practice long enough for it to become a habit. For instance, you will be interacting with your adult son or daughter and treating him or her as an adult, no matter how he or she acts. In the long term you're increasing your level of education incrementally, not just by going to meetings, reading books, and seeing a counselor yourself, but also by gradually changing how you talk to your adult child and also how you provide help.

He or she may not get it at first. Your addicted adult child will likely continue his or her habits, which is acting like a minor, long after you have already started to treat him or her like an adult. Now that you know better, though, you can persist until he or she also understands the actual relationship and is able to adjust behavior, something that may not happen until after he or she has actually dealt with the addiction.

These incremental changes tend to be baby steps, but they are important progress in the right direction. We sometimes refer to this course of study and practice of new learning as a journey. It is an expedition of new learning and practicing new behaviors that build on themselves through time. Eventually you get to the point of actually letting your child go... into his or her **full adulthood**.

At a certain point on your journey of change, you will see your adult child reacting in a more positive, healthy way, and you will know it's because of the changes you have made.

Often there is a flash of insight when you realize that *things are changing because of the changes you have made.* Things are not yet where you want them to be, but this glimmer of change reinforces your hope. At this point, you can shift from operating on faith that the process will work to feeling more certain that you are on the right path. This might happen at any point along your journey, but trust that it will.

Finally, you're *leading* your relationship with your adult child instead of having an addicted loved one leading you.

A Framework: Eleven Principles of Family Education

While the first step of your education is to read this entire book, the most important lesson to learn is that there is hope. As long as you continue to move forward by educating yourself and taking new actions when necessary to help your adult child, there is hope.

These eleven principles of family education provide a framework for your journey:

1. There is a curriculum to your loved one's recovery from addiction, and you can learn it.

2. Your loved one's recovery is not an event. It's a process through time, a journey.

3. Your loved one's journey is one of emotional and spiritual growth.

4. This journey is a marathon, not a sprint.

5. Your loved one's journey of growth invites you to focus on your own journey of growth.

6. Despite appearances, you have no control over your loved one's journey, only your own.

7. Your loved one's journey is not your journey.

8. Your journey forces you to face and confront some unpleasant realities of life.

9. You are not alone on your journey, and all the help you will need is available. But, you must seek it.

10. The further you go on your journey, the more it helps your loved one.

11. You can get to a point on your journey where, no matter

what your loved one does, you will either know what to do, or know where to find out what to do.

Study and Learn

Some of the things you're going to learn in the short term will feel overwhelming because you won't be able to perform the behavioral changes you want to make at the same pace as you're learning about them.

Our culture often confuses learning with *having information*. There is an old saying:

> *"You don't really know it*
> *if your behavior doesn't show it."*

Typically, you will have more information than you can put into action. Therefore, your ability to practice patience will be a key to your sense of sanity during this journey. You may well be frustrated during this learning process, so it will be helpful to listen to others who are going through the same things as you but may be further along in the journey.

This is where groups like PAL can be so helpful. Parents can share information and support with other parents. They understand your pain and your journey in a way a counselor may not be able to, and they are eager to share what they have learned to help you avoid the pain they had to experience. This can make your journey easier.

As you learn and grow, you too will be able to help others. Because you will be able to share your learning with them. It might not seem like it right now, but you will find this is true, and it can be a "magic moment" for you, even if it is not an official one. To know enough to be able to help others is a great feeling.

Changing behavior, however, is not simply as easy as knowing better. It can be, but often it takes time and practice to change your actions to match what you have learned. Because humans are habitual creatures, we must have a long-term goal to be able to make new habits. Look at how long we have been practicing the old habits!

Until now, it's all been black and white and you didn't have to think about boundaries or limits or how much or how little you would help. Up until now in your mind, you were still legally responsible for an adolescent, so you had to help your child without limits all the time, every time.

After your child reaches the age of eighteen, there may still a history of this sort of response. Maybe he or she has been pulled over and charged with possession of drugs two or three times. You can see that your adult child is *not* moving on. You can tell by his or her language that you are expected to provide bail again, and you wonder why he or she is not taking responsibility and not changing. The reason? *He or she doesn't have to.*

There is a lot to learn about the best way to talk to an adult child because it is different than the best way to talk to an adolescent. With adolescents and children under the age of eighteen, you are the authoritarian and you can tell your loved one what to do. He or she has no choice. You are responsible for your adolescent child and so typically you do not give him or her many choices.

When interacting with an adult, however, you may suggest choices, but he or she decides what to do. This process of giving suggestions and allowing your adult child to make choices is an important part of helping him or her learn how to make good choices. Of course, your loved one will make some bad choices along the way, but as the old saying goes:

"How do you learn how to make good choices?
By making bad choices."

If you try to control too much, you will experience rebellion, most often as a diversion to facing the real issues. "I will do something bad to get you to try to control me, so I can get angry over your controlling and react to it by getting high" is one of the common games your addicted adult child will play.

With your new education from books, groups, counseling, experience, etc., you will see this game more clearly and learn how to respond in a way that is not only better for you, but also benefits your adult child.

Through time, you can learn to recognize the most common games and decide whether you want to play. You can refuse to play, or you can play with a variety of different responses. This new learning gives you more choices in multiple situations, and that helps you figure out what works best for your loved one.

Disempowerment is having only one choice as your reaction, and, as we know, one choice is no choice. This is the legacy of habitual behavior.

Habits can be very helpful because they allow you to do complex things, such as drive a car, without having to think about all the details. The other side of that coin, though, is that unexamined habits, such as automatically saying "yes" to every monetary request made by your adult child, can be very limiting; again, one choice is no choice.

Let's say nineteen-year-old Johnny calls from jail. You've bailed him out once before, but this time you want him to experience the consequences so that he can learn from them, since he did not, apparently, learn from them the last time. As is often said in Alcoholics

Anonymous meetings, "If nothing changes, nothing changes."

So the conversation might go something like this:

Johnny: "Mom, you've gotta come and get me. You can't believe how bad it is down here! There's drug users and rapists and murderers and child sex abusers in here with me. You need to get me out of here!"

Mother: "What do you want me to do?"

Mom's response is a departure from how she would treat someone younger than eighteen and probably different from the way she responded to Johnny's previous request for instant assistance. She is making him take responsibility for asking for the help he wants. Yes, this may seem obvious at first, but you can begin to see how much it changes the conversation.

Johnny: "Mom, I want you to get me out of here!"

Mom: "How do you expect me to do that, Johnny?"

Johnny: "I don't know, Mom."

If Johnny was an adolescent, his mother would jump right in with the answer. Now we're letting Johnny think about the situation and take responsibility for finding his own answers.

Mom: "I don't know, either."

Johnny: "Yeah, but Mom, you got me out before. Just do it again!"

Mom: "Yes, I did bail you out last time and look how well that turned out. You just got in trouble again. I'm not going to do that again."

At this point, Johnny will probably give all kinds of excuses, perhaps doing his best to use blame and guilt to encourage his mother to bail him out again or get angry.

Johnny: "I thought you loved me! It wasn't my fault this time! This is wrong! Do you know what could happen to me in here? And it will all be your fault!"

These are all words that you probably have heard before. This time you can just listen patiently, and when he's done, continue to treat him like an adult and repeat your request for him to take responsibility.

Some parents have found it useful to use a **metaphoric model** to help learn how to communicate with an adult child. Instead of thinking about talking to their adult child, the parents approach the communication as they would if they were talking to, for instance, a third cousin who was fifty-five years old. So in this case, the fifty-five-year-old is a metaphor for your son or daughter.

Obviously, Johnny is not your third cousin nor fifty-five years old, but this model can help keep you on track by giving you perspective. Simply ask yourself, "How would I talk to my fifty-five-year-old cousin Fred?" compared to "How I would talk to my nineteen-year-old son, Johnny?"

For instance, if your drug-using cousin Fred called and said, "I'm hungry, and I don't have any money" would you say, "I'll be there as soon as I can with some food or money?"

Chances are you would reply, "Wow, Fred! How did you get into this situation?" or "Are you hungry enough to get help for your drug problems?" That's how you talk to an adult.

So this metaphoric model helps you learn how to talk to your adult child more like you were talking to a friend: "How can I help you?"

This can certainly be hard to swallow. We must continue to remind ourselves of this new perspective and make changes accordingly.

By refusing to take responsibility for your adult child, he or she now has to either get someone else to take responsibility or begin to take responsibility for him or herself.

Your primary goal is to refuse to take responsibility for your adult child's actions and inactions. This is one of the major things you're learning.

You're also learning that, in some cases, by doing less, you're actually doing and accomplishing more. This very likely will go against your natural parenting instincts, which is to be expected.

When it comes to accomplishing a worthwhile goal, such as saving your adult child from drugs or alcohol, doing less does not make sense to some people, especially those who have a strong work ethic. That's also why there's quite a bit of work and practice in learning these new behaviors and why many times this new behavior won't feel right at first.

Some people might call this "**tough love**." Although I don't particularly like that term, it does have some value. I like to say that we call it "tough love" because it's tough on mom and dad.

When you really look at the situation objectively, you will see that your children are survivors. They always were, and they always will be. So it's your vision of your adult children as being adolescents (seventeen, sixteen, fifteen, twelve, ten, whatever age you picture your son or daughter to be in your mind's eye) that makes it tough for you to let them take responsibility for themselves; especially when they're making such a mess of their lives.

You can overcome this all-too-common dilemma by accepting the truth that *how you see your son or daughter in your mind definitely affects the decisions you make about how to help.*

This won't change immediately, because it is a habit that you have learned over time and will likely have to change the same way. Parents report that becoming aware of the false impression of their son or daughter's age and changing it each time their loved one comes to mind is hard work, but is necessary to change that habit.

Changing How You Help
Not only do you need to make the commitment to change how you help your addicted adult child, *you must tell him or her you are doing so.*

This in itself can be frightening, but it is equally or even more empowering. You are changing your relationship with your loved one in a way that is good for him or her and good for you.

Doing it can be daunting, but once you do it, you will realize how much power you really have.

As a parent of an addicted loved one, you and your adult child will travel a journey of fits and starts. That's why it can be very helpful and productive for you, at some point, to have a talk with your adult son or daughter.

The conversation might be something like this:

> As we've told you before, your mom and I have realized that we've been treating you like a child for far too long, and we're going to start treating you like the adult you are. We have been learning this through reading books, attending meetings, and seeing a counselor. As we mentioned before, we hope that you will understand and forgive us for making the mistake of treating you like a child for too long.

So you will see changes in how we help you. We will always help you because we love you. We are, however, learning how to give you specific, precise help instead of unconditional help. We're doing this because we believe it's best for you. It's hard on us, and we know it's also hard on you. But if you do not change, if you do not grow, and if you do not start taking more responsibility for your decisions and your actions, you will be a failure as an adult. And, we will feel like a failure as parents. So that is why we are doing this.

Magic Moment #4: Committing to Changing How You Help:

"I am going to treat you like the adult you are, and adjust the way I help you accordingly."

Sam's Story

Sam was a twenty-five-year-old man attending his second treatment center in Tucson, Arizona, for prescription opiate abuse and heroin. His parents came to one of our PAL groups in Phoenix and seemed to be fairly quick studies. They were motivated and hungry to learn. Sam's father began to learn about the concept of treating his son more like an adult child instead of an adolescent.

Early on, they realized that Sam's mother saw her son, in her mind, as being fifteen years old, while his father, in his mind, was seeing Sam as twelve. So in this case, the father was actually being less rigid with his son than his mother.

This is an exception. From my experience, about

ninety percent of the time, fathers are tougher on their sons. This isn't right or wrong, that's just the way it is. We use the term "ten percenter" when referring to this exception to the general rule.

While at the treatment center, Sam would call his parents from Tucson every day and complain about things at the center.

"There are murderers up here," Sam would say. "There's a child abuser who is a registered sex offender here." One time he reported, "Some guy showed me a knife and threatened me."

Because they were seeing him as a youngster, Sam's parents believed his reports and were very scared for him. Sam wanted to come home, and he also wanted to see his girlfriend, who lived in Phoenix.

Once they adjusted their perspective about their son and began to see him as a twenty-five-year-old adult, they had some fears, but not the same sort as if he were fifteen or twelve.

Now they began to question Sam more and talk to his counselor at the center. Sam's counselor assured them that these are the types of things an addict says when he wants to leave because he is having to face the pain of treatment.

In the end, Sam did complete the program and come home, although he did relapse and use drugs upon his return.

His parents were happy that he had at least completed the program, though, and asked Sam to sign up for an outpatient program. Sam agreed to attend and did indeed go, so his parents allowed him to live at home. But then he used again.

With their new knowledge, his parents had asked Sam to sign an agreement known as a Recovering Person's Plan (an example of which we share later in this book) to which he had agreed. In the plan, he committed to leaving the house if he used drugs again. So when they discovered that he had violated their agreement, they asked him to leave the house, and he did. The plan included an option to go back to in an inpatient treatment facility. Sam refused and hit the streets.

This never could have happened if his parents had continued to see him as being twelve or fifteen years old. Who could put a child out on the street? If they had continued to treat him as a boy, Sam would likely have continued to manipulate them for weeks, months, or years, and his addiction and behavior would have likely worsened.

Instead, Sam stayed at his girlfriend's apartment and called his parents daily to complain about his life. Eventually, his girlfriend got tired of him not working or getting a job, so she moved in with her parents. Somehow Sam talked them into letting him move in, too.

After a few weeks though, his girlfriend's family asked him to leave and he wound up living in his car. Sam continued to try to manipulate his father, texting him messages such as, "I've never been so depressed in my whole life. I don't know what to do."

Previously, his father would have come up with a solution for Sam, but now that he was more educated about working with an addicted loved one, he texted back, "I believe you. I believe in you, and I believe you can figure out a way."

After a couple of days of Sam dangling bait and parents not taking it, he finally got tired of living in his car and called his parents. "I want treatment," he told them.

They had never heard those words from him. So he entered an inpatient treatment program and, at last report, his parents saw a noticeable difference in his attitude and behavior.

Sam continued to try to manipulate his parents, but his actions didn't have the same effect. He seemed to be listening and learning, too, and began talking about moving into a halfway house after completing inpatient treatment. That is a very positive sign, as most recovering people want to go home after getting out of inpatient treatment.

You can see how replacing over-helping with precise helping can be scary and painful, but in the long run, so worthwhile. This story also illustrates how seeing your addicted loved one as an adult, instead of whatever younger age you were picturing him or her, is vital to also changing your behavior and, ultimately, his or hers.

It also illustrates that it may take a couple of tries before your addicted loved one understands and accepts that things are now different. This is why it is so important that you not only change your perspective, you must change your habits and behavior accordingly.

Cutting Financial Strings

You may have heard about children tied to their mother's apron strings. There are other strings too, such as those that control puppets. When dealing with an addicted adult child, it's important to eventually cut those strings.

Sometimes financial strings are obvious, and sometimes they aren't. It's important to learn how to identify strings, and then plan the safest ways to cut them.

I like this quote:

> "Only when every string was cut, did Pinocchio
> have a chance to become a real boy."

An excellent way to cut strings and treat your loved one like an adult is to create written plans and contracts, much like you would do in a professional situation between adults. These plans and contracts help clarify the situation and what is expected of each party.

They can also remove much of the potential emotion caused by the coming change. By using these tools, your addicted loved one can view the agreement as being the authority; rather than a parent.

Sometimes you will fill out these plans and forms yourself, such as with the plan for cutting financial strings. Other times, your loved one will participate in setting goals and establishing agreements that must be made so you and your adult child can move ahead.

Financial strings are often the most important control issue between parents and their children.

Some say they are the only strings, and for many families it's true. There are parents who are constantly bailing out their adult children, and many of their offspring don't really know whether they can take care of themselves and doubt they will ever have a successful life as an independent adult.

This is something an adult needs to know about him or herself.

Parents cut financial strings in order let their adult children know that they can take care of themselves. The only way to do that is to go ahead and *actually* cut the financial strings, but first you must identify those strings.

Because this is such a common and predictable problem, it is important to create a form that lets you "divide and conquer" the mass (some would say the "mess") of financial strings between you and your adult child.

Once you are ready to commit to cutting financial strings with your addicted loved one, it is time for Magic Moment No. 5. It might occur either before or after you complete the form. This is one form you can complete without the participation of your addicted loved one because it is only for assessment.

Magic Moment #5: Committing to Cutting Financial Strings:

"We have been inadvertently preventing you from learning financial responsibility, something every adult must know. That is not our intention, so we are going to cut the financial strings that have held you back."

On the next page is an example of a completed Financial Strings Checklist. A blank copy of this form for your own use is available at www.palgroup.org.

Financial Strings Checklist

Adult Child's first name: **Cody**

True Age: **19** Age I had seen him/her in my mind's eye: **10**

1. Adult Child's living situation (home, apartment, etc.):

In our home.

2. Adult Child's transportation situation:

He has use of our 2nd car.

3. Adult Child's auto insurance situation:

He's on our plan at $45 per month, is supposed to pay us each month.

4. Adult Child's health insurance situation:

He is on our family plan.

5. Adult Child's money/savings/assets/trust fund situation:

No savings account. No money, No trust fund.

6. Adult Child's cell phone situation:

On our family plan at $10 per month, is supposed to pay each month.

7. Adult Child's present employment situation:

Unemployed at this time.

8. Adult Child's past employment history:

10 different jobs, none lasted over 2 months.

9. Amount of money Adult Child owes us from loans:

Approx. $1,500.

10. Adult Child's personal belongings in our home/other place we're responsible for:

Clothing, papers, personal items.

11. Adult Child's school & other expenses:

Not in school at this time.

12. Adult Child receives this type of mail at our home:

Old bills and advertisements.

Once you have filled out this checklist with your adult child's situation, you will have a much clearer view of all the ways you might control him or her. You'll also see the many ways he or she may be manipulating you, or when and how much help you actually do provide.

As much as you may resent the financial drain on you, your son or daughter may also actually resent the control you have because of your financial oversight.

These sorts of strings are not good for you or for your loved one, who must accept responsibility for his or her life; especially financial responsibility.

How One Mom Explained Cutting Financial Strings to Her Son

Dear Son,

I want you to know that I've been seeking education on how to help you resolve your various problems. I'm learning from parent groups, peers, and counselors with the goal of learning what's best when it comes to me providing you with financial help.

Don't worry: I will never stop helping you. But I'm learning how to stop treating you like you are still a child and, instead, how to help you like the man you've become. I've learned that if I help you financially too much, it may help you in the short term, but it can actually end up hurting you in the long term.

That's because over-helping an adult child financially can prevent him from ever becoming an independent person. I'm learning how my financial help for you can be more precise. Ironically, this new way of helping, although limited in the short term, can actually benefit you greatly in the long term.

It won't be easy for me to stop giving you unlimited financial help, which is how parents are supposed to help their young children. You are an adult now, so I will be limiting the financial help I give you. This will take time and practice, but I believe it's the right thing to do for you and is absolutely necessary for me as a loving parent who wants to help you become self-sufficient.

Change can be very frustrating, especially when the reasons for change are not explained. So if you want to know my motives for what I'm doing or not doing when it comes to helping you, please feel free to ask. If I can't totally explain my reasons to your satisfaction, I will give you the names and contact information for the professionals who have been guiding me through these changes, and you can ask them.

I love you and will never give up on you. I want you to be successful as an independent, self-supporting, and responsible adult, and I believe that is your goal as well.

Love,
Mom

Once you see the importance of cutting financial strings with your adult child, now you are ready to take the actions necessary to make it happen.

Having a Parents' Plan outlining your goals can be a very helpful next step.

Developing a Parents' Plan
If there is any disagreement within the family about the best way to help your adult child, it can be helpful to formulate a written plan.

Because it's so important for parents to maintain a *unified* position when helping their loved one, it is vital they come to agreement on the details of such help. This is where a written Parents' Plan can come in handy.

Whether or not you are currently in contact with your adult child, you can use this plan to document your agreement on what *you* are willing or able to do and not do. This is another form you can fill out without the input of your loved one.

Remember, these are your limits and goals. The consequences at the bottom of this plan apply to you. For maximum benefit, you must sign the form.

As you can see, completing the Financial Strings Checklist is a big help as you formulate your Parents' Plan. It helps you see very specific situations where your adult child needs to take responsibility.

Establishing this plan is an important but challenging step for you to take, so you might want to ask for professional help with this task. A counselor or recovery coach can assist you in filling out the plan.

A blank copy of this form for your own use is available at www. palgroup.org.

A completed example can be found on the next page.

Remember, too, that these plans and checklists can be updated, edited, tweaked, added to, etc. to fit your needs as they evolve. Some people find it helpful to work with the documents this way, while some people only need complete them once.

This plan can be very helpful to your family as a guide to helping your adult child when he or she is not quite ready to ask for help or when he or she is not in contact with you.

Parents' Plan for Helping Our Addicted Loved One (ALO)
Example

Date: 8/8/14

My/Our Name: Mary / John Smith

ALO Name: Cody

Rel. to me/us: Son

ALO's Present Living Situation: Living in our home

My/our Vision for ALO's Eventual Living Situation: His own Apt. or Renting a House with Sober Roommates, stable employment and working a solid Recovery program.

Specific Actions* Parents will Take With Target Dates for Completion
*Change = Awareness + New Action

1. Have Cody complete a Recovering Person's Plan with us by 9 / 1 / 14

2. Take Cody off our cell phone plan by 12 / 1 / 14
As a gift, offer to buy Cody a Cricket phone with the payment plan in his name and pay the first month charges by 12 / 1 / 14

3. Stop paying Cody's auto insurance on 1 / 15 / 15
   Take our name off of the title to Cody's car by 1 / 15 / 15

4. Tell Cody all debts owed to us are now forgiven A.S.A.P.

5. Ask Cody to begin paying rent of $200 per month beginning 1 / 15 / 15

6. Take our name off of Cody's checking account and stop helping him balance it by 1 / 15 / 15

We/I agree to these consequences should this plan not be followed through:
See a personal counselor once a week. Or agree to enter "Bridge to Recovery" inpatient program for codependents in California. Or attend Al-Anon and get a sponsor within one week. Or attend three PAL, Al-Anon or Nar-Anon groups each week. Or attend the "Breaking Free" program in Phoenix when next available.

Mary Smith

Parent Signature

John K. Smith

Parent Signature

Like the other forms shared in this book, this plan is deceptively simple, yet it is extremely powerful, as it forces both you and, perhaps, other key members of your family to come to agreement and set goals with real target dates.

Just as in any forms of commitment for your addicted loved one, the consequences section of the Parents' Plan is particularly important.

Whatever the consequences for you as parents are, they must be specific and measurable. The more severe they are, the more motivated you will be to follow through on your established goals. Notice that the consequences are designed to help educate you, not punish you, if you're not able to follow through on the goals you have agreed upon.

Still, they need to be achievable. Make sure as you write your plan, that your goals are helpful but not unrealistic.

This plan can be part of your transition from a *parent-to-child* relationship to a *parent-to-adult child* relationship. Still, it's very challenging for you as loving parents to take a tough stance while trying to help your adult son or daughter.

Why Establish Extreme Consequences?

All drugs, including alcohol work the same way: they cause the brain to feel a sense of well-being. They do this artificially because they are all chemically similar to normal brain chemicals, which is why psychologists use the term, **mind-altering substances**.

The short-term effect of drugs, including alcohol, is intense and gives the user a short-term strategy to deal with day-to-day issues; much like the approach a child might take rather than the long-term thinking an adult must use.

Over the years I've heard the many reasons addicts tell me they need to take drugs and alcohol:

"It helps me focus."

"It helps me concentrate."

"It helps me calm down."

"It helps me relax."

"It helps me escape my inner critic."

"It helps me shut off my brain."

And on and on. One young man who was just finishing high school said, "My drug helps me succeed. I can't do my job or my homework without it, and I would be a failure without it."

I've also heard, "It helps me feel less anxious, less depressed. I feel more normal, more alive."

The addict may have started out partying and having fun socializing, and drugs or alcohol were just a part of that. But somewhere along the way, too many perceived "benefits" came from such use, and now the person has made it an indispensable part of life.

As discussed in the previous chapter, he or she may have entered the third stage of addiction, the desperation phase.

Denise's Story
The use of drugs to cope with life's problems is clearly demonstrated by some messages a forty-five-year-old client named Denise left on my answering machine.

A marijuana smoker who also had other addictions including alcohol, Denise left me two voice-mail messages on the same Sunday several years ago. Here is her first call:

> *Good morning, Michael. It's Denise. It's about ten a.m. I'm just giving you a ring because, oh my gosh, I'm wrestling with it today. I have no feeling of self-worth and can't find any hope. Stupid suicidal thoughts are flowing through my mind. You know, "What's-the-use," that kind of thing. It's really awful when I'm in this sort of place. I just don't know what to do. I get the sense that my higher power's telling me, "You really aren't worth much." I keep praying and asking for the perfect plan to help me, but I just can't seem to get an answer. So here I am managing my life and the world by myself. Yeah, I can call my AA sponsor, but it all looks pretty stupid, these little support groups, right now. When it's all said and done and I get done talking, I still have to live with myself. Why bother? An hour after the talk, I still have to deal with the same thing I had to deal with before the talk. I just don't understand it, and it isn't helping. Anyway, as you can tell, I'm really wrestling with it today. I'm down to my last fifteen hundred dollars; that's all I have separating me from, well, I don't know what's next, and I don't see any hope of that changing.*

Her second call came two-and-a-half hours later:

> *Michael, Denise again. It's about twelve-thirty. By now, you've gotten my earlier phone message, and how I was feeling. Since then, I stopped by a friend of mine's house, got a dime bag of pot and smoked a joint. Now my attitude about life is: Wow! This is exciting. I've got more than a thousand dollars in the bank. My higher power cares about me, and I feel totally inspired to tell myself to go out and make some*

money. That's the thing with pot. I was practically suicidal two-and-a-half hours ago. Now I feel like I can deal with it all. I called you back because I want you to see the contrast, this crazy paradox I live with. When I haven't been smoking any pot, I get into that downward spiral. I'm telling you this so that you can see both sides of it. This is how it is for me with this pot in my life, this addictive behavior. Also, in the past two days, I just felt driven to go to a bar and go home with some guy. It's like I'm acting out, but thanks to the pot, I managed to stop myself from that. Anyway, I'm just giving you a view from my perspective so you can really see where I'm coming from. I just want you to see how I experience this.

This conversation is a dramatic example of why we need to establish extreme consequences. Notice how quickly Denise was able to feel better about herself and her life by using drugs; in this case marijuana. Denise went from hopeless to hopeful in a matter of minutes.

This story helps illustrate the challenge you can encounter when trying to "talk sense into" a son or daughter using drugs or alcohol. Most people are using their drug of choice to cope with life's ups and downs. It is a challenging task indeed to talk an addict into giving up something that makes him or her feel better and be motived to enter recovery. Often it is when consequences, whether planned or not, catch up to an addict, that he or she realizes that drugs or alcohol really aren't helping.

> *As is often said in the recovery field: "People don't change when they see the light, they change when they feel the heat."*

Another example of demonstrating this point can be found in the book *Smoke and Mirrors* (Dorothy Marie England, Forward Movement Publications, 1995):

"Extreme consequences are necessary if reality is ever to break through. The pain of consequences must outweigh the relief the addictive behavior brings. In our society, we do not handle pain well. We are taught to be sympathetic; when others hurt we hurt with them, so it is in our own interest to prevent others from hurting or to ease their pain as soon as possible if they do hurt.

We are taught that pain is bad; if someone hurts we should help him or her get relief. While this teaching was helpful in the case of the Good Samaritan, it is not helpful in the case of addicts. In this paradox-filled disorder, preventing or lessening pain is the most dangerous, destructive thing one can do.

Addicts need to be jailed when they break the law. They need to be confronted when they violate trust. They need to be left where they are when they pass out, even if it is in the car on a cold night. They need to reap any mental, psychological, biological, and spiritual consequences of their behavior short of death. Only through extremely painful or multiple painful consequences does reality crack denial, giving addicts an opportunity to see their disease and make movements toward recovery. Pain is what gives addicts and those who suffer with them a spiritual edge."

Yes, addicts need motivation to get help, and we are beginning to see why they need so much motivation. From their standpoint, they are giving up some tremendous benefits from their drug or alcohol use. As mentioned above, in most cases, the pain resulting from their drug or alcohol use must be greater than the benefits derived from that use.

Growth Pain or Wasted Pain?

There's going to be pain if a person makes changes, or, for that matter, if a person doesn't make changes.

There is a lot of pain associated with addiction because of all the areas of life that are negatively affected by it. Family members also go through their own pain as a result of trying to help their addicted loved one.

As a parent, if you keep trying to help your adult child the same way you always have, you will have the same type of pain you have already experienced. If that pain motivates you to seek help, then it was not wasted pain. If it provides the motivation for positive change, that makes it **growth pain**.

Wasted pain just keeps coming around, and no positive change occurs as a result of it. Sometimes this is called "squirrel cage pain" or "hamster wheel pain" because there is movement, but none of it moves you forward. If you are going to feel pain, it might as well be productive.

Take a moment and think about the pain you have felt regarding your addicted loved one. What kind of pain has it been? What kind of pain would you prefer?

Growth pain provides motivation for parents to get educated and for addicts to change their lives.

Regardless, it's still very important to understand that addicts will need to be clean and sober and in their right mind so that they may be helped. Further, they must be willing to be guided in their changes by other people.

Such guidance best comes from someone outside of the family, and that can be a bitter pill for parents to swallow, but it's one of the ways parents must change their viewpoints in order to truly help.

Getting Unstuck
Even after your loved one attains sobriety, he or she may continue feeling stuck. Often this happens when parents continue to treat their adult child as a youngster and the child obliges them by acting like one.

This creates a cycle of no change. Nothing's changing, and as we know from Alcoholics Anonymous, "When nothing changes, nothing changes". Inadvertently, the parents are actually helping the addict avoid change and stay stuck. This problem may not be immediately obvious, and the solution may not be, either.

The answer is that you must move ahead regardless of your addicted loved one's action or inaction. You may be asking yourself, "How can I move on without my son or daughter?" It may seem selfish, and it is, but it's a **healthy selfishness**. Each parent getting help for him or herself is giving a wonderful gift to his or her adult child.

Parents get angry because of their addicted adult child's slow progress. Part of that anger is at themselves for having allowed a loved one to manipulate them into helping slow down that progress.

Parents may also realize that somehow their adult child can continue manipulating them to help his or her *avoidance of change.* This can continue with no end in sight. It's frustrating because parents don't know exactly how this happens; but it's happening, and it hurts.

As more and more time goes by with no change in sight, avoidance of change can become a dangerous problem. With education, parents can come to understand this mystery and see how they can make changes, no matter what their adult child does.

Using drugs and alcohol not only lets your adult child stay stuck, but also medicates his or her depression that can come from not having a productive life. It's important for parents to see that their children do have goals and dreams for a better future, but those goals and dreams are usually suppressed.

A common fantasy is that the journey to adulthood just naturally happens. It doesn't. It takes conscious effort, and parents often do not know how to help their children with this complex task. With no formal rite-of-passage education, preparation or ceremony, they themselves may have never been formally taught about it.

Fortunately, although it comes later than the legal threshold of eighteen, this forced transition from being an addict to accepting adult responsibilities can finally serve as your child's rite of passage.

In PAL groups and private sessions, I often ask parents, "Are you feeling stuck, too?" I ask that question so they can become aware that they may also not be moving on with their lives, because their adult children are stuck. It's not helpful to stay stuck with them.

As long as your addicted loved one is not asking for help, he or she is still in an addict's winter, but you want to make sure you do not stay there with him or her.

Parents can benefit from seeing a counselor to help them deal with their children's issues and also with their own issues from the stress of trying to deal with an addicted adult child. It is quite common for your children's problems to create issues in your marriage, your work, your parenting, and all other areas of your life. These are the types of things a counselor can help you resolve.

Feelings of grief and frustration are also quite common during this time, and it is extremely hard to resolve them without professional help.

Moreover, when a parent gains a measure of resolution for their own painful emotions, it benefits the adult child who has the addiction.

Sometimes you may experience a sudden *thaw*, and you want to believe that spring has arrived and your dreams for your adult child as well as their own dreams can now bloom. But without proper preparation, it may be just one more hope unrealized, one more disappointment.

Depending upon the family, its history, the age of your addicted loved one, and his or her particular journey, there may be many years of disappointment from being stuck in never-ending winter, and many disappointing promises of successful long-term recovery that have not come. Or there might be a short winter and a true spring right away.

What determines the story? There are too many factors to list, but one of the first great lessons is that parents can influence their adult sons and daughters, but *they cannot control them.* They may need to learn this lesson over and over again until they finally grasp the depth of this truth.

We pray for spring, as we educate ourselves to practice new actions and begin to realize it's all we can do, yet *this is all we need to do for our loved ones*. The other thing we need to do is something we do for ourselves; at some point put our attention back on our own needs and the needs of the rest of our family.

This does not mean we are not helping our addicted adult child. It only means we are not living our life totally for him or her, like we were when they were true children. Now that they are eighteen or older, they are free. Part of that freedom is the freedom to fail and the freedom to be hurt, as well as the freedom to succeed.

Learning this new lesson is a long-term goal, requiring a journey that is probably longer than you had hoped, but will make sense when you realize it affects every area of your addicted loved ones' life.

Therefore, recovery from addiction must address every area of a person's life as well. We're talking about friendships, spirituality, love relationships, family, life-balance, recreation, career, self-improvement, education, sexuality, moral code, life purpose, etc. There is no bigger curriculum than that of *life*. This is the curriculum of recovery.

Someone once said that most people live their lives in a very superficial way, like a water-bug gliding along on the top of a deep lake. In recovery, that depth must be explored. The prospect of diving into a deeper level of self to gain self-awareness and self-knowledge is not always the most welcome of human goals. It can be a frightening notion to realize that "the journey into self requires the presence of another." In addition to being a family member, that presence can also be a friend, counselor, sponsor, coach, clergy member, etc.

Changing Habits Takes Time
You already have a history with your addicted loved one that includes many interactions and habitual responses to those exchanges. You now need to be willing to change some of your past habits so that the outcome may also change.

This poem, from an unknown author, captures why habit both helps and challenges us all:

I am your constant companion. I am your greatest helper or your heaviest burden. I will push you onward or drag you down to failure. I am at your command.

Half of the tasks that you do, you might just as well turn over to me and

I will do them quickly and correctly. I am easily managed. You must merely be firm with me. Show me exactly how you want something done. After a few lessons, I will do it automatically.

I am the servant of all great people and the regret of all failures as well. Those who are great I have made great. Those who are failures I have made failures.

I am not a machine but I work with all of its precision, plus the intelligence of a person. Now you may run me for profit or you may run me for ruin. It makes no difference to me. Take me, train me, be firm with me and I will lay the world at your feet. Be easy with me and I will destroy you. I am called Habit.

Angela's Story

Angela had a twenty-year-old son, Sean, who lived at home and smoked marijuana. She started attending PAL meetings because of how frustrated she was with Sean. He would not seriously look for a job, stayed in his room during the day playing video games, and would go out at night with his friends. Sometimes Sean would stay out all night and come home early in the morning. Angela did not know where he was getting the money for his drugs or for the incidental expenses a young man would have living at home, even though he enjoyed free rent and meals.

After attending several PAL meetings, Angela revealed to the group that she was becoming aware of all the energy she was putting into trying to motivate her son. She would try and wake him up in the morning, try to find potential employers for him, offer to take him places for interviews, etc. She began to see more clearly the bad habits of over-helping she had developed over the years. Even though she had learned about the concept of helping an adult child "help himself" instead of doing it for him, she admitted she felt powerless to change her ways.

She also became aware of the unseen habit of picturing twenty-year-old Sean in her mind as a fifteen-year-old. She was beginning to understand that the old unreal picture in her mind was a hidden factor in her decision-making process when it came to helping her son.

She was becoming aware of not just habits of action, in other words, trying to control her son's actions for his own good like he was a fifteen-year-old child, but also habits of thinking, like seeing Sean as a fifteen-year-old instead of the twenty-year-old man that he had become.

It would be hard for her to change her mental picture, especially when Sean was acting like a fifteen-year-old. But that is the suggestion she received from other parents at her PAL meeting.

For many years, parents have been developing a habit to see their children and treat them a certain way. In the instances we are discussing, they have been treating them as underage children, something they've had eighteen years to practice. What a habit! It's an understandable one, but one that needs to be addressed to allow children older than eighteen to become adults.

The first part of changing a habit is becoming aware of what that habit is. The second step is practicing a new behavior you have chosen to replace it. You must practice the new behavior over and over again and eventually, through time, the new behavior becomes a new habit.

Changing your habits forces you to pay more attention to what you are saying and doing, and why. You will learn to identify certain habits that work against your best intentions. One example could be giving your addicted son or daughter money for daily living expenses when you know or suspect he or she will use that money to buy drugs or alcohol. This sort of habit actually helps your addicted loved one avoid changes you wish he or she would make.

Your new habits, such as saying "no" to unhealthy financial requests, may feel uncomfortable at first. That's not because they're wrong, but because they're unfamiliar. Those old habits, even though they're not helping your loved one, may feel comfortable to you because they are familiar, but that doesn't make them right.

As you get more and more comfortable with your new habits and start seeing the positive results in your adult child's behavior, they begin to feel normal. That just means you have developed new habits. It will take a little while, though, so be patient with yourself.

If you find yourself reacting in an old way even though you're committed to reacting in a new way, you are not a failure. The fact that you've even noticed the difference is a sign that you are actually succeeding. If you find yourself reacting the old way, simply begin practicing the new response *after* you've reacted the old way.

After awhile, you will notice that the amount of *time* between when you're aware and when you are able to react the way you prefer, gets shorter and shorter. That's the true measure of your progress. With persistence, patience, and trust in your new knowledge, the time will come when you catch yourself *in the moment of your old reaction* and then you will be able to correct in the moment instead of having to go back and correct after the moment.

Even if after you have successfully adopted the new habit, you may react the old way occasionally, perhaps when you've been pushed too far. Don't get discouraged, because ultimately the more you practice your new behavior, the more it will become your automatic response.

New Parent Roles

Now that you are treating your addicted adult child like an adult, your parental roles have changed. No longer are you playing the old habitual family roles we learned about previously: Enabler, Codependent, Rescuer, Enforcer, Ignorer, Punisher, Controller, Jailer, Lecturer, Pretender.

Now you are becoming a:
• Partner
• Encourager
• Listener
• Boundary Setter
• Positive Communicator
• Cheerleader

These words imply that you are doing less for your addicted loved one, so they can do more.

These are just words, however. For instance, "boundary" is just a word until it is tested. The challenging task of acting your new role takes a bit of instruction, practice, and time. Who will you pick to help you learn your new role? It's best to ask for input from several sources, such as a substance abuse counselor, Al-Anon sponsor, PAL Group member, or recovering person.

In your new role, what new, different behaviors or actions will you practice when it comes to relating to your adult child? Here are some examples from parents:
• Stop telling my son what to do.
• Listening more and talking less.

- Telling my daughter I believe in her and know she can be successful in her recovery.
- Admitting I can't help anymore and suggesting professional help.
- Saying "no" to requests for money.
- Setting boundaries such as, "You need to move out by Monday."
- Spending more time taking care of myself and my needs.
- Seeing a counselor.
- Going to PAL and/or Al-Anon meetings.

As you practice your new habits, the biggest thing you need to remember is that you are now dealing with another adult, not a child.

Because you have learned to stop giving instant answers to requests from your son or daughter, you can take the time to stop and think about how you would treat other adults in this situation, and act accordingly.

Recognizing Triggers
First, let's define what **triggers** are. Triggers, or hot buttons, are merely temptations. We all have temptations in life. For instance, "I want another donut, but I'm on a diet." "I need to quit smoking, but a friend of mine just lit up."

Triggers can simply mean temptations that you can see, hear, smell, taste, or touch. In one way or another, your loved one is experiencing an association that reminds him or her of whatever good feelings came from whatever he or she was using or doing.

Sometimes addicts and alcoholics use the word triggers almost as an excuse. It may sound something like this: "I couldn't help myself; I was triggered."

Yes, temptations can be strong, and that is why people have the resources of their **recovery program**, which has all the instructions and tools needed to have a fulfilling life without drugs or alcohol.

Once again the addict can see that it is up to him or her to put in the time and effort to build a strong program so that he or she can deal with the temptations. There will always be triggers in life, but the more often you experience a trigger and make the right choice, the weaker the effect of the temptations in your life.

The term "triggers" can also be used in a broader sense to include associations family members have made through previous experiences. For example, a son talking to his mother in his child's voice asking for help can be a powerful association that becomes a trigger for a mother to treat her adult child like a youngster. This is one of the most common situations I see when working with families who have an addicted son or daughter whom they are trying to treat as an adult.

Once parents become aware of such triggers, they can watch for them and recognize them for what they are.

Whether an addicted loved one is using these triggers intentionally to keep using drugs is really beside the point. As you have learned, their effect simply isn't one you or they want anymore.

Parents can learn to identify their own problematic triggers that cause them to repeat old behavior we sometimes call enabling. As we learned in an earlier part of Spring, enabling means giving someone help in the short term that ends up hurting him or her in the long term. This is a big issue in recovery and a big part of new learning that parents need help with.

For more information about enabling, it may be helpful to again review that section earlier in this same chapter. As you continue to learn and grow, information you have read before may have new meaning for you.

We know that the addict's dedication to his or her addiction affects the whole family. That's why we call it a *family disease*. It's not that the family caused the addiction, but that the addict's problems affect the whole family.

A silver lining behind the dark cloud of addiction is that each person in the family has an opportunity to identify areas of potential personal improvement for him or herself.

Playing the Role
Let's say your addicted loved one picks a fight with you. Now you have more awareness of the dynamic of your interaction and know that one of your new choices is to refuse to fight. You may also notice that your adult child's actions also brings up some of your own past issues. That presents you with an opportunity to see a counselor to help you fine-tune your own communication skills.

So how do you respond?

Role-playing can be a very helpful tool as you learn a new way to speak to your adult child, particularly when you are changing your own role in interacting with an adult child as opposed to raising a youngster. I highly recommend role-playing, however, with a professional who is adept at the practice.

Role-playing new language, word choices, reactions, and "scripts" can be very helpful. Below are suggested sentences parents can use, sometimes over and over, in their new conversations with their sons and daughters.

We call these **"gems"** and provide a handout of them for PAL Group participants (they are available for free on the Web site at www. palgroup.org):

- "I love you and I will always love you, no matter what."
- "I believe in you."
- "I'm pulling for you."
- "I'm praying for you."
- "I know you're going to beat this problem."
- "You are an adult now, and I hope someday you can forgive me for having treated you like a child for too long."
- "You're an intelligent person, and I believe you will solve this problem."
- "How can I help you help yourself?"
- "I will never detach from you, but I am detaching from certain problems of yours so I don't rob you of the self-esteem you will get from solving your problems yourself."
- "You can always ask me for help. But, please be specific about your request. I'm trying to stop reading your mind, thinking for you, anticipating your words, and offering what I think you need."
- "When you ask me for help, I will consider your request, discuss it with those I trust, and get back with you very soon."
- "My love for you is unconditional, but my help for you is not. I don't want to make the mistake of giving you the kind of short-term help that ends up hurting you in the long-term."
- "I am educating myself so I can learn better ways to help you."
- "I am learning to see the difference between growth pain and wasted pain."
- "I will always love you and always help you. But my help may be limited to prayer, letters, words of encouragement, hugs, or sharing a meal together."
- "I'm not listening to your words, I'm noticing your actions."
- "I prefer to not speak with you at this time. Please communicate with me through texting, e-mail, or letters only. Thank you."
- "I have resigned from my job as your rescuer."

• "I'm not going to argue with you; let's agree to disagree."
• "I'm asking you to act your age instead of your urge."

Just reading these phrases gives parents hope that there are some new things they can say to help change their relationship with their adult son or daughter. But that hope is not enough. They also need to practice these new communication skills in order to make them a habit. When counseling parents, we often spend time practicing role-playing. We call this "safe practice" yet it can definitely help parents feel more ready for "real world practice".

It will take some time before your new way of relating and communicating with your son or daughter becomes an ingrained habit. I often quote Albert Einstein on this point:

"Repetition is the mother of all new learning."

The changing of habits is a lot of work, but there is no substitute for it. I submit that your willingness to do the drudgery of repetition over and over again through time is evidence of your love for your child.

This need for repetition and reinforcement for new learning to take place is one of the most important reasons for the existence of the PAL support group. There, parents can receive new information and practice new ways of reacting and communicating with their adult son or daughter. By going to the meetings, they can receive as much repetition and reinforcement as they need to be successful and ultimately change old habits that are no longer working and replace them with new, constructive habits.

There is a lot to learn in spring, much of which may seem obvious to you once you know it. It is an exciting time, one in which it may indeed feel like the sun is finally shining on you.

SUMMER

"The summer sun shone round me."
— Robert Louis Stevenson

Summer occurs after a successful spring, when there has been a period of progress, and things seem to be getting under control.

Summer is that period of time when your loved one is in recovery. He or she has accepted help and is receiving, or has received, some form of treatment for his or her addiction. Consequently, you are feeling relief and are also more hopeful.

Your adult child may be getting help at a treatment center, through a substance abuse counselor, a support group like AA, a halfway house, jail, or some combination of these resources. After initial treatment, he or she is often released to some kind of transitional living. He or she must get outside help because no one can do this alone.

Wherever he or she is in the process of recovery, no matter how he or she may be struggling, you now can feel greater hope about the situation. Maybe now you can work on having the relationship with your adult child that you have been hoping for.

Your progress and that of your adult child may not follow a straight path of going from discovery of the problem through to a successful adult life and relationship with you. Although they are, hopefully temporary, there may be many setbacks and bumps in the road.

Treatment Options

There are a number of common **treatment options,** or levels of care, available to addicts today.

There are many factors that will determine which option is best for your adult child, as well as which one he or she would be willing to enter. In addition, there are the practical realities of insurance coverage and financial limitations.

Here are some of the most common treatment options:

Detox: This medical setting is for the gradual removal of addictive substances from the body. The time necessary usually varies from two to seven days and prepares a person for inpatient or outpatient treatment. It's important to note that detox is *not* treatment.

Residential Treatment, also known as "**Inpatient**" or "**Rehab**": This is a situation where your loved one will be housed twenty-four hours a day, seven days a week. The customary length of stay usually varies from thirty days to six months.

Partial Hospitalization, also called "**PHP**": This is a form of treatment where the person does not live at a center, but attends certain treatment activities at the center, commonly six hours a day, five days a week, Monday through Friday. An addict usually commits to attend PHP for one to four weeks.

Intensive Outpatient Treatment, "**IOP**": This is another form of treatment in which the person does not live at the center but attends treatment activities, usually two to three hours a day for three to four days a week. The length of time commitment to IOP is commonly around two months.

It's important to note that there are many variables and combinations of the above options that are appropriate for each person. For instance, many will need all four in the order shown, while some may only need the last one.

All of these options traditionally incorporate twelve-step programs such as Alcoholics Anonymous, Narcotics Anonymous, Cocaine Anonymous, etc. as part of their treatment regimen.

After Treatment Options for Sober Living
After treatment options may actually begin while your loved one is still in outpatient treatment or partial hospitalization. That's because they aren't living at the center that provides the services, but they need to be surrounded by recovery resources in their living environment.

The term **sober living** is common terminology for all types of sober housing. Here are some options:

Halfway House: This is a generic term that refers to a wide range of sober living options. It might be a home with multiple bedrooms, or an apartment building with multiple units. Some halfway houses have a lot of structure, while others have minimal structure. What they have in common is rules and consequences for breaking them. For instance, the use of alcohol or drugs most often triggers an automatic removal from the house.

Because of his or her history, if your loved one needs more structure and discipline, a more structured halfway house with more rules would be best. There are managers who enforce the rules and may even drug test, impose curfews, and require attendance at a specified number of twelve-step meetings a week.

Three-quarter House: This term is not used very often, but it implies a halfway house with less structure and fewer rules. It relies on the maturity of the residents to provide their own discipline. This option usually includes a manager who has less oversight.

Sober Living House: This term applies most commonly to a sober living environment with little structure and rules. That's because each person has reached a level of maturity and personal responsibility, so they are only seeking sober roommates. There might be a manager with minimal oversight or no manager.

Transitional Living: In addition to sober living, this is another generic term commonly used to imply and include any of the above choices, although it most commonly refers to halfway or three-quarter houses.

Janel's Son Gets Help

About a month after Janel cut Ernie's final financial string, she got a phone call from him from jail.

He had been picked up on a drug charge. He also reported, with sadness in his voice, that his friend from the streets had overdosed on heroin and died. Ernie said he was serious now about his recovery and wanted to enter a treatment center upon release from jail. Naturally, Janel was happy to hear this, but she had heard it before. Because of her new learning, she was cautiously optimistic.

A couple of weeks later, Janel got another phone call from Ernie. He was released from jail and sitting in his probation officer's office. He told Janel that, true to his promise, he was on the waiting list of a local county-run drug and alcohol rehab program. It could be a week or two, however, before a bed would be available for him.

So he asked Janel, "Mom, can I come home until a bed opens up at the treatment center?"

Janel later reported to our group that, without a lot of thought, she said, "No." Whereupon Ernie spat out an expletive and hung up the phone.

Janel says that she would never have been able to say "no" without having gone through those previous experiences of gradually cutting those financial strings with her son. She got strength from her courage to make baby-step changes in how she was helping her son.

This is a wonderful example of both baby steps and incremental learning through time and experience. As it turned out, Ernie's probation officer found a halfway house for him, and he lived there for about two weeks and then entered treatment and completed the program successfully.

A Long-Term Project
Summer is what you experience when you see your addicted child has finally accepted help.

But it's early in the process of a long-term project, and you might be wondering, "How long will this last?" or "Will it work this time?"

Summer is obviously a more hopeful season than spring but there are many hurdles to conquer and quite a bit of work the addict needs to do to have a successful, long-term, recovery. Your son or daughter may be getting help for his or her addiction, but still has far to go. There are many habits that support the addictive lifestyle, and these habits take time, practice, and much work to change.

In the season of summer, you hope that your addicted child will learn to be more independent. He or she may have been somewhat independent before, but the chances are that, at times, he or she was also dependent upon you financially and/or was dependent on drugs or alcohol or on a love relationship. Summer marks the season when a recovering addict attempts to prove through time, to him or herself and to you, that he or she can face life on life's terms without having to return to chemical use for stress management.

It is common for parents to have the experience of multiple summers as well as multiple winters. The test remains the same: "Do they keep getting help and then relapsing?" Just as important for parents, do we keep coming back to winter when they do? Remember, the promise of this book is no more winter. That will occur because of the changes *you* make.

I propose that if there is a long history of help and then relapse and then more help and then more relapse, in most cases there is a love interest, or a family member, or a friend, who is involved in accidentally helping this process continue. This situation is commonly referred to as enabling, as we have discussed.

We're not suggesting this help-to-relapse is intentional. On the contrary, my experience is that this help is motivated, rightly or wrongly, by love. It needs to be pointed out that by over-helping an addict financially, you may be helping fund a relapse.

Completing Residential Treatment (Rehab)
When your son or daughter has completed a schedule of residential treatment, whether it be thirty, sixty, ninety, or 180 days, it will be around the time of your adult child's discharge when your worries will tend to increase. This is to be expected because during treatment he or she was safe and constantly surrounded by help.

Parents typically get more worried when their loved one completes some form of treatment and now must test their ability to remain drug-free without the support surrounding them in the treatment setting. The support of peers in recovery, along with professionals helping them, is an important part of inpatient treatment, and that support will be missed upon completion. Hopefully your child has learned how to replace the support *team* they are losing.

Will your son or daughter be successful in maintaining his or her sobriety without such substantial support? That is the challenging test that occurs when your child leaves treatment to re-enter regular society. This is a time where typically parents want to take more control and yet know they need to let go. This is a testing time for both parent and child.

Using Adult Coping Skills

As we discussed in Spring, recovery gives us a proposed list of adult coping skills, skills your loved one will learn as a byproduct of staying clean and sober and *working the program* of his or her choice, through time. "If you don't do the work, you don't get better," is an old recovery saying.

When your child is finally willing to fully give him or herself to this recovery work/life-skills training, you will notice certain adult coping skills developing before your very eyes.

You will witness your loved one learning how to:
- Practice more honest communication.

- Earn money legally.

- Be more reliable in keeping commitments.

- Agreeably accept guidance of authority.

- Be patient and delay gratification.

- Give up control to authority.

- Control his or her anger.

- Make responsible decisions.

- Take responsibility for those decisions.

- Be more generous and less selfish.

- Set boundaries on their generosity with others.

Daily and Weekly Recovery Activities

The way you can know when your loved one is really doing the work of recovery is by his or her actions. You will see him or her doing such things as:

Attending twelve-step meetings. There are a variety of twelve-step meetings available today. Alcoholics Anonymous was the first and the most famous. All of the other twelve-step meetings use a variation of the original twelve steps but essentially they are identical. For instance Narcotics Anonymous uses the word "drugs" in the place of the word "alcohol". There are similar small changes in Pills Anonymous, Marijuana Anonymous, Heroin Anonymous, and Crystal Meth Anonymous.

All of these self-help groups are free, and all of them offer sponsorship. A sponsor is a member of one of these groups who has completed working all twelve steps with the help of his or her sponsor. Sponsors do their work of helping other members on a volunteer basis and, by helping others, sponsors are completing the last step, or step twelve, of their own twelve-step work.

Sponsorship is so important to any of the twelve-step programs that, if there were no sponsors, the program would be virtually useless. That's how important the relationship is of one man helping another or one woman helping another along the journey of recovery.

Finding a sponsor he or she can work under. Typically, at twelve-step meetings there will be many more members who are available to sponsor others than there are people asking for a sponsor. All someone seeking a sponsor needs to do is go to their choice of a twelve-step meeting and ask for a sponsor.

This, of course, brings up all kinds of trust and control issues for recovering people, even though they know they need to let someone else guide them. Again, underlying issues crop up that need to be addressed for a recovering person to move ahead.

Working through these issues (preferably with the help of a counselor) is one of the most important steps your loved one takes toward accepting responsibility for his or her life.

Completing the twelve steps with a sponsor is a critical part of recovery. The sponsor's job is to guide and lead a person through the twelve steps. He or she will direct the recovering person at a certain pace, with the goal of doing a thorough job and completing the steps in the correct order. It is, in itself, a rite of passage from addict to adult.

Ending unhealthy friendships is also an important task to help an addicted person stay clean and sober and have a successful life without drugs or alcohol.

Many people will resist giving up certain friends because of loyalty. Whether the loyalty is to the person or to the drug is a valid question, but one for your adult child to ask him or herself. One suggestion is to ask the addict to decide which unhealthy friends (those still using drugs or alcohol) he or she wants to retain and which friends he or she chooses to release. This may be part of your loved one's Recovering Person's Plan. (See page 155)

With friends your adult child doesn't care to retain, he or she can either call and say goodbye or just never resume contact; and delete those phone numbers from his or her cell phone.

The friends your loved one wishes to keep can be called or contacted by text or email and told something like this: "I want to keep you as a friend, but I cannot be around you at this time because of my recovery. As my friend, I know you will understand and I'm asking you to be patient. When I have enough clean time to feel strong in my recovery, I will be back in contact with you. Until then, God be with you, my friend." It can also be wise for the recovering person to get a new phone number.

Taking necessary prescribed, non-addictive medication may also be important. For instance, it is common for an addicted person to have depression, bipolar disorder, ADD, or anxiety issues.

It is worth noting that there are some medications that, although legal, are addictive. For instance, medications for ADD, anxiety, and pain all have valid medical applications, yet some are nonetheless addictive, much like alcohol. This can present a challenge to someone struggling with addiction, so it is important that recovering people take non-addictive legal prescription medications instead.

Obviously, a medical professional who is part of your loved one's care team will prescribe any necessary prescription medications. That professional needs to be informed about your adult child's addiction issues before prescribing any medicines and, ideally, have a background in working with addiction issues.

Building friendships with others in recovery is absolutely critical. Friendship is a very important part of recovery. Recovering addicts need to learn how to pick better friends. Friendship with other recovering addicts should be a priority. Twelve-step programs, treatment centers, counseling groups, and churches all provide opportunities for a recovering addict to meet another.

I often use the term "the brotherhood and sisterhood of recovery".

This brotherhood and sisterhood does not and cannot replace family. It is, however, a powerful agent of change to help addicts become better family members, which is a very challenging and difficult task for family members.

We are not asking recovering men and women to give up their existing friendships with healthy people. In early recovery, however, it is very important that the recovering addict build a support network of clean and sober recovering friends. Some people have such friends, and some have none. It will be these friends that your son or daughter picks to spend time with and develop trust with.

It is these friends that your child can talk to and be more honest with about challenges and needs in order to stay clean and sober. A sponsor can be considered such a friend. It's recommended that each recovering person have a goal of developing at least five clean and sober same-sex friends who are in recovery.

It's important to note that Alcoholic Anonymous' *Big Book* is very clear about the potential pitfalls of male-female relationships in early recovery. If you do not own this book already, it is truly helpful for understanding the nuances of addiction.

The wisdom of having five same-sex friends is simple. When an addict is being tempted to relapse, he or she knows the importance of calling someone, like his or her sponsor or friends, talking with him or her, and getting help to avoid relapse.

Although family members would like to be in that helping position, there are many potential reasons for an addict to be less than fully honest with a loving family member. For example, there may be secrets involving other family members or past behaviors that are easier to discuss first with a friend or sponsor rather than another family member. In an ideal world, he or she might be able to be totally honest. When it comes to talking about certain sensitive subjects, family members may be at the bottom of the list of who the addict could be comfortable with.

Having a friend you can talk with about any subject is truly helpful. Having five friends gives a person the opportunity to reach out for help from five sources instead of only one; which would be the case if the person only had a sponsor.

Doing regular recreational activities with recovering friends may sound frivolous, but it is another important way for recovering people to build new, positive habits. The recovering person must be able to have fun on a regular basis. By doing so with other clean and sober recovering addicts, such activities help build the trust necessary to develop the clean, sober friendships that were mentioned before.

AA's *Big Book* talks about how we in recovery absolutely insist on having fun. Obviously, it means clean and sober fun. This issue of having fun is extremely important, and especially so for the young people of today.

What sorts of things can they do for fun? Here are just a few:

Some Sober Leisure Activities

Acting	Basket weaving
Attending boxing matches	Bicycle riding
Attending wrestling matches	Bird watching
Attending auto races	Boxing
Attending arts/crafts shows	Caring for cats
Attending auctions	Caring for dogs
Attending car shows	Caring for houseplants
Attending lectures	Caring for pet birds
Attending plays	Caring for snakes
Attend political activities	Coaching sports
Ballroom dancing	Collecting antiques

Collecting coins
Collecting stamps
Cooking, baking
Country line dancing
Crocheting
Cross country skiing
Designing clothes
Dining out
Doing aerobics
Doing carpentry
Doing genealogy
Doing gymnastics
Doing isometrics
Doing jigsaw puzzles
Doing macramé
Doing metalwork
Doing needlepoint
Doing needlework
Doing string art
Doing yard work
Downhill skiing
Drawing
Driving
Exercising
Fishing
Flying a kite
Gardening
Getting into conservation/ecology
Getting into photography
Going backpacking
Going boating
Going bowling
Going camping
Going canoeing
Going four-wheeling
Going to barbeques
Going to concerts
Going to garage sales
Going to movies

Going to museums
Going to plays/theater
Hair styling
Hiking, walking
Home decorating
Horseback riding
Hot air ballooning
Hunting
Ice-skating
Jet skiing
Jewelry making
Jogging
Joining a book club
Joining a church
Joining a health club
Joining a school club
Kayaking
Knitting
Learning and using a ham radio
Learning archery
Learning art appreciation
Learning astrology
Learning astronomy
Learning mechanics
Learning judo/karate
Learning sign language
Leather working
Listening to music
Listening to talk radio
Making arts and crafts
Making ceramics/pottery
Making movies
Marksmanship
Mentoring
Model making
Motorcycling
Mountain climbing
Newspaper reading
Officiating basketball

141

Officiating soccer
Officiating softball
Officiating volleyball
Painting, oil or acrylics
Painting, watercolor
Parachuting
Parasailing
People watching
Playing backgammon
Playing badminton
Playing billiards, pool
Playing bingo
Playing board games
Playing Bocce Ball
Playing bridge
Playing cards
Playing checkers
Playing chess
Playing computer games
Playing cribbage
Playing croquet
Playing darts
Playing dominoes
Playing drums
Playing euchre
Playing flute
Playing golf
Playing guitar
Playing Hacky Sack
Playing handball
Playing hearts
Playing horseshoes
Playing in a band
Playing lawn games
Playing miniature golf
Playing piano
Playing Ping Pong
Playing racquetball
Playing shuffleboard

Playing soccer
Playing softball
Playing squash
Playing spades
Playing strings
Playing Uno
Playing video games
Playing/watching baseball
Playing/watching basketball
Playing/watching football
Playing/watching Frisbee
Playing/watching hockey
Playing/watching tennis
Playing/watching tetherball
Playing/watching volleyball
Playing water polo
Practicing calligraphy
Practicing mediation
Practicing Tai chi
Practicing yoga
Quilting
Refinishing furniture
Relaxing
Reminiscing
Restoring automobiles
Rock climbing
Roller-blading
Roller-skating
Reading
Running marathons
Sailing
Scuba diving
Sculpting
Sewing
Shopping
Sightseeing
Singing
Singing in a choir
Skateboarding

Skydiving
Sledding
Snowboarding
Snowmobiling
Snow skiing
Social dancing
Square-dancing
Stargazing
Stenciling
Studying Astrology
Studying Astronomy
Sunbathing
Surfing
Swimming
Synchronized swimming
Taking children on outings
Taking school classes
Talking on the phone
Teaching a skill
Tobogganing
Traveling
Tubing
Using a Nordic Track

Using a Stair Master
Using a stationary bike
Using a treadmill
Visiting amusement parks
Visiting aquariums
Visiting art shows
Visiting coffee houses
Visiting exhibits
Visiting fairs
Visiting parks
Visiting the YMCA
Visiting friends
Volunteer work
Watching television
Water skiing
Weight-lifting
Window-shopping
Weaving
Woodworking
Working crossword puzzles
Working with copper
Wrestling
Writing

Attending counseling sessions is optional yet strongly advised. Individual counseling sessions can be quite helpful to recovering people, especially in early recovery. Twelve-step groups provide opportunities to interact with other recovering people, obtain a sponsor, and build healthy friendships, but none of that substitutes for the help that individual counseling can provide.

For this reason, it is recommended that, if at all possible, the recovering person find a counselor he or she can trust to help him or her deal with emotional issues. The counselor can thus round out and add to the recovery team of sponsor,

143

recovering friends, and in some cases, a minister or other spiritual leader.

Reading recovery books also can be quite helpful. It is highly recommended that people in recovery read AA's *Big Book*. It has been around over some seventy years and is filled with proven wisdom.

For many recovering people, reading the Bible or other religious books is also quite helpful and appropriate. In addition, the recovering person can ask his or her sponsor, counselor, or recovering friends for suggested reading materials.

Attending church or being part of a religious community is optional but strongly suggested when your loved one is ready to explore his or her spirituality. The AA program and all twelve-step programs are based on helping people awaken spiritually and then relying on God to guide them in their life. Attending church or being part of a religious community is not for everyone, though. I suggest you allow your adult children to explore their spirituality at their own desired pace.

Planning for Re-Entry

Re-entry is the difficult transitional period of time when a person leaves residential treatment (also called "inpatient"), to re-enter society, whether they've been living in a facility for thirty days, a year, or anywhere between.

This is a difficult time because a person must adapt to the stresses and pressures of a clean and sober life (which feels like ordinary life to others) after getting used to the lessened pressures and stresses of life in rehab.

Re-entry planning, also referred to as aftercare planning, is critical for every recovering person's long-term success because re-entering society to live a sober life demands difficult change from a population with a high resistance to change.

The recovering person also, in essence, is starting a new life, leaving the known for the unknown, which is always challenging.

By anticipating the particular challenges of change for each individual, you can formulate an aftercare plan that takes into account the amount of time a person might need to adjust to the changes of a new life, one without drugs or alcohol. Considering the concept of **rate of change** (which is simply how fast changes occur) is absolutely necessary. This is a time to go slowly.

Without such foresight, the recovering person (and parents, who want things back to "normal" as soon as possible) might be tempted to rush this adjustment process and accidentally invite failure. In addition, the recovering person may be very impatient and not yet fully aware of the devastating effects of rushing the process.

My experience is that most graduates of rehab programs who fail to stay clean and sober, will relapse within the first twelve months after leaving the protective rehab environment. This happens either because they fail to write an aftercare plan before they finish rehabilitation, or they fail to follow the aftercare plan they have written.

In developing an **aftercare plan**, there are many factors to consider, including:

- How old is the person?
- How many relapses has he or she had?
- How many years has he or she been practicing the addiction?
- How problematic has his or her lifestyle been?

- How many times has he or she been in rehab?
- Have there been any periods when he or she demonstrated clean and sober, independent, mature, and responsible living?

In most cases this information will be used to complete an aftercare plan that fits your loved one's particular situation. It is usually completed with the assistance of a counselor.

Understanding Aftercare

Aftercare is when you successfully complete inpatient rehab and transition to a sober, more independent life. Rehab provides an impatient care program and upon leaving, you must replace it with your own aftercare program. It's like getting out of the hospital with your legs in casts; you will still need crutches and physical therapy for a period of time.

An addict's aftercare program is perhaps the most critical part of any successful long-term recovery because it exponentially increases the chances of the recovering person's long-term success. It is critical because the recovering person is learning how to live clean and sober while experiencing his or her full freedom.

If a recovering person resists having an aftercare program, you need only ask him or her, "Do you want short-term or long-term recovery?" Aftercare is an important part of helping recovering people practice new habits of sober living that become part of their lives.

Aftercare Planning

Here is a proposed "menu" of activities a recovering person might want to include in his or her aftercare plan. Notice it suggests activities plus practical details about time and frequency of each. A goal without a timeline is not a goal, it is a wish.

❑ Sign up for an Intensive Outpatient Program (IOP)
   By when?_____
❑ Enter a halfway house
   When? _____ For how long?_____
❑ Find a sponsor
   By when?_____
❑ Develop sober friendships
   How many?_____ By when?_____
❑ Go to 12-step meetings (AA, NA, CA, etc.)
   How many per week?_____ Starting when?_____
❑ Perform daily prayer or meditation
❑ Perform service work at meetings
      (volunteer clean-up, make coffee, etc.)
❑ Have face-to-face visits with sponsor
   How many per week?_____
❑ Make phone calls to sponsor
   How many per week?_____
❑ Attend aftercare group meetings
   How many per week?_____
❑ Attend group counseling sessions
   How many per week?_____
❑ Go to marriage counseling sessions
   How many per week?_____
❑ Go to individual counseling sessions
   How many per week?_____
❑ Attend worship services
   How many per week?_____
❑ Attend Bible study
   How many per week?_____
❑ Recreational activities with sober friends
   How many per week?_____
❑ Other:

An aftercare plan is sometimes called a family agreement when family members are involved in the recovery process (which is highly recommended and most common). This plan helps the recovering person resist the temptation of taking too much control of his or her life too soon after completing inpatient treatment.

Instead of letting an "addict mind" make decisions, a sane and sensible plan written by the recovering person, with input from others, guides him or her during those first critical twelve months after leaving rehab.

Because of its importance, this plan is ideally completed just before discharge by your recovering loved one, key family members, and treatment center staff. If staff is not available, I highly recommend contacting an addiction counselor or recovery coach for help in completing this plan.

It's important during the completion of this plan that your loved one is involved in the discussion of the decisions, because it's about his or her life. On the other hand, if he or she is fighting every suggestion or, conversely, giving into every decision too easily, it could be a sign of a problem.

Ideally, you want to see the recovering person being open to suggestions from treatment staff and also willing to accept your boundaries and consequences when it comes to your wishes. At the same time, he or she needs to be able to freely discuss his or her own wants and needs. His or her ability to participate effectively in this process is a sign of true maturity.

Following is an example of an aftercare plan I have used with clients who were completing their 30 days of inpatient treatment. This example shows some sample suggestions. I highly recommend, however, you use the form your treatment center provides.

The sample aftercare form on the next page gives you the structure for your recovering loved one's life after inpatient rehab, along with a number of typical options and choices.

There are certainly more options and choices out there, but this gives you some idea of the kinds of choices recovering people commonly make. The number and type of options each person chooses will depend on his or her particular situation, another reason it's important to create this plan with a professional.

This plan is important because it's not just about drugs or alcohol; it is about your son or daughter's life. He or she will want to have more control over it than you, and you may want to have more control than he or she prefers, so this process is ripe for contention. Again, a professional will be a great help.

If you have these issues in writing, and everyone worked together to create the plan and signed it, you have something tangible you can refer to, if necessary. It can resolve arguments about what was agreed to and resolve any breach of the agreement. The agreement also is an objective authority that is not you, not a treatment professional, and even not your son or daughter, helping drain the emotion out of a potentially explosive situation.

The example plan on the next two pages includes multiple options for each section. You will pick those that work for your situation, or you may choose different options altogether. The example is just intended to give you some ideas.

You can find a blank version of the form you can print for your own use at www.palgroup.org .

Aftercare Plan / Family Agreement
Some Examples for a Variety of Situations

Date: *June. 12, 2013*

My most preferred living situation: *My parent's house. My house. Move in with a sober friend. Rent an apartment. Enter a halfway house.*

Sobriety/abstinence actions to take: *Go to ninety 12 step meetings in 90 days. Attend 4 AA meetings each week. Obtain a sponsor within 3 days. Call sponsor daily. Report any cravings Immediately to family and friends. Choose an AA home group in 7 days. Take a service position at a 12 step meeting.*

Family actions to take: *Attend or organize a Family Night one night per week. Plan a "date night" with my spouse once a week. Plan or attend a monthly family outing. Make amends to those whom I have wronged. Spend at least 1 hour of regular special time with each of my children individually each week.*

Social actions to take: *End all relationships with friends who use drugs and alcohol. Restore relationships with at least 5 clean and sober friends or develop at least 5 healthy same-sex friendships. Go to a fun recreational outing at least once each week with friends who do not abuse drugs or alcohol. Attend AA/NA social functions.*

Spiritual actions to take: *Read the Bible or another spiritual book at least 10 minutes each day. Meditate at least 5 minutes each day. Attend an organized worship service of some type every week. Join a men's or women's Bible study, class and attend weekly.*

Work actions to take: *Because my old job is not a safe environment, I will seek a low-stress job by updating my resume and submitting at least 10 applications per week until I find a position where I can use my skills and build my work experience.*

Emotional actions to take: *Attend individual counseling weekly. Attend marriage counseling every two weeks. Always be rigorously honest. Complete steps 4 & 5 with sponsor within 60 days.*

Legal actions to take: *Contact attorney within 5 days. Attend court on the 17th. Complete community service within 6 months. Pay off all fines that are due within the year. Successfully complete my probation.*

Physical actions to take: *Stop eating junk food. Start eating breakfast. Get 6 - 8 hours of sleep each night. Exercise at least 3 times per week. Take all prescribed medications. See the dentist at least every six months or more as needed.*

CONSEQUENCES: *If I use any mind-altering substance that has not been prescribed or take it other than prescribed: I will enter a 6-month rehab program immediately OR go to a sober living situation OR enter intensive outpatient OR lose all financial help for 1 year.*

Date: _____

_____
Recovering Person's Signature

Date: _____

_____
My Family/Friend Signature

Transitional Living

One choice for the recovering person who needs to develop more mature coping skills or has shown an inability to remain clean and sober after a previous treatment attempt, is some form of transitional living. Choices include: 1) halfway house, 2) three-quarter house, and 3) sober living house. These were discussed previously in detail.

These three forms of transitional living provide time for adjustment to sober living by offering a safe, supportive, hard-to-manipulate, sober environment in which an addict can grow and mature. Transitional living provides recovering people more time to adjust to the extra pressures that come from not only living life as responsible adults, but doing so without the use of alcohol or drugs to cope.

Most often, recovering people enter transitional living after completing an inpatient program. Other times, recovering people might go into transitional living because they can't afford inpatient care but need some kind of recovery help. Another time might be when he or she has been in treatment previously, perhaps years ago, and feels like he or she is slipping and needs a refresher. Recovering people might also go into a transitional living setting because they think they don't need treatment, but still might be open to some sort of assistance, including low-cost housing. Another time this path is helpful would be when people have just been released from custody.

It can be very helpful for an addict with a long history of addiction, to transition into a halfway house after inpatient treatment. Then, after a time, move into a less structured halfway house (sometimes called a three-quarter house), and then eventually move to a sober living house which provides little or no external structure.

This type of growth through small incremental steps, with each step having less overt structure and rules than the previous one, works very well because it allows a person to gradually take responsibility for providing his or her own discipline and structure. It's rare though, for someone to choose to grow slowly.

A halfway house provides a half-step toward the goal of full re-entry. In a halfway house, people are expected to obtain low-stress employment and pay rent, sparing them the immediate pressures of a high-stress job, family and school, or trying to please someone.

While living in a transitional facility, the recovering person's non-working "free" time can be spent visiting family members as well as going to meetings, seeing a counselor, working with a sponsor, developing at least five sober friendships, doing fun recreational activities weekly with sober friends, developing spiritual practices such as church, Bible study, morning devotions, and getting used to honesty, accountability, discipline, and responsible living. They are building new, healthy habits for a life without the crutch of drugs and/or alcohol and the enabling behaviors of mom or dad.

The recommended time for staying in transitional living usually varies from ninety days to a year, depending on the individual needs of the person.

Writing a Recovering Person's Plan

Another type of plan that is similar to the aftercare plan, is the Recovering Person's Plan. Unlike the Aftercare Plan, which is designed for an addict completing treatment and willing (hopefully) to continue to work on his or her recovery, the Recovering Person's Plan can be used for a wider range of situations.

The plan lists the goals your son or daughter wants to accomplish, the steps for cutting strings, and the consequences if he or she relapses. It includes specific actions to take and target dates by which they will be taken.

Remember: *Change = Awareness + New Action*

This is one of those times to put that equation into action.

The following recovering person's plan can be a helpful tool, but remember, it's not your plan, it's your loved one's plan. You can have input into the plan, especially if he or she is presently living in your home or is planning on returning home. In fact, that is when this plan is most commonly used.

Allowing your recovering adult child to live with you creates a touchy issue and an emotional one as well. It's best to address this issue and attain clarity with your loved one about it. When your child reaches his or her age of independence at eighteen, your home is not his or her home anymore. Your loved one is living in your home and should eventually be able to obtain his or her own home.

Yes, he or she is welcome in your home, but it is *your* home and your loved one needs to follow *your* rules. The Recovering Person's Plan is a helpful tool for documenting agreements between parents and an addicted adult child.

You and your loved one, whether he or she is in recovery or still struggling with addiction, can work together using the example that follows as a guide to negotiate the goals and terms of the plan. This might be a good time to ask for professional help to mediate and negotiate the plan. A substance abuse counselor or recovery coach can really help with this process.

Unlike the Aftercare Plan example in this book, which offers multiple options for each section, this example shows how a completed plan might actually look. You can find a blank version for your adult child's use at www.palgroup.org.

Recovering Person's Plan
Example

Date: 10/21/2013

My Most Preferred Living Situation: My parent's house.

My Plan "B" Living Situation: My friend Jake's house or brother Mark's house.

1. Move out of my parent's home by 2/21/14.
   Open a savings account by 10/25/13.
   Obtain Driver's License by 11/15/13.

2. Obtain employment by 11/7/13.
   Save up at least $3,000 by 2/15/14.
   Pay outstanding $180 fines by 1/15/14.

3. I agree to promptly take a drug or alcohol test at any time.

4. Attend appointment with psychiatrist for evaluation by 11/1/13.
   Allow parents to control and dispense ALL of my medications, starting right now and continuing until I move out.

5. Attend initial appointment with Counselor by 11/3/13.
   Take full responsibility for controlling my temper outbursts. Be willing to be videotaped during my outbursts so I can see and hear myself the way others do.

6. Contact Probation Dept. and ask for revised payment plan by 11/15/13
   Pay court bill of $270 by 12/31/13.

7. Complete the following list of household chores every day:
   Make my bed.
   Pick up things off the floor in my bedroom.
   Put my dirty clothes in the hamper.
   Wash dinner dishes and put them away.
   Take out the trash in the kitchen.

Consequences I agree to, if I use any mind-altering substance not prescribed, or not taken as prescribed:

Within 24 hours, I will move out of the house and into a halfway house with my parents paying the first month's rent.

_____   _____
Recovering Person's Signature   My Family/Friend Signature

155

Keep It Simple

In writing a Recovering Person's Plan, it's important to keep the plan clear and simple. If the plan is too complex, it can be difficult to track results and make it too easy for your adult child to ignore. He or she does not need any reasons to not comply. Clarity is paramount to completion and to keeping everything calm and respectful.

Below is an example of a plan written by parents for their twenty-one-year-old son Stephen, who was allowed to live in his parents' home. This plan has good intentions, but is problematic for two main reasons: it is too complex and gives too many chances after a failure to comply.

Dear Stephen,

Ever since you left rehab, I advised you that I would be writing down our expectations and our commitment to you. I am sorry we have not done a better job in helping you to become independent. It is our desire at this time to make a commitment to you and to assist you in becoming an independent adult. I believe that you are fully capable of functioning independently and that your strong determination will be an asset in your ability to make this transition to independence. You have a strong personality, you are intelligent, and you have many skills that will help you be successful at whatever you do.

This document is designed to let you know our expectations for you as long as you are living with us or we are supporting you financially. When you turned 18, we were no longer responsible for you, financially or in any other way. However, as your parents, we do feel we will always be responsible to you. This means we will always love you. We will pray for you. And we will support you as we feel it is appropriate.

For the past three years, your mom and I have chosen to pay all your living expenses as well as your phone, insurance, medical, as well as occasional spending/cigarette money. I even offered to pay for a college class. The following will detail what we are willing to commit to you in the future with the following conditions.

If you choose to go to school:
We will pay for your first class and books needed for that class. If you want to continue in college, we will help you gain financial assistance.

Conditions:
You must be meeting a curfew of 10:30 PM Sunday through Thursday and an out-of bed time of 9 AM on Monday – Friday. This does not mean moving to the couch and sleeping. The one exception to this will be if you attend an agreed-upon support group and you all go to a restaurant afterward. We will pick you up no later than 11 PM.

Curfew Friday and Saturday is 12:01 AM as long as you remain drug and alcohol free. Out of bed time for Saturday is 10 AM. If you abide by this and are on time for 1 month, we will adjust to 12:30 AM. If you continue to be on time for a second month and are drug and alcohol free, we will adjust this to 1 AM. January 6, move curfew to 12:30 AM. February 6, move curfew to 1 AM

You must treat us with respect. We will do the same (i.e., no foul language, no yelling, door slamming or other disrespectful behaviors). After one warning, the consequences for curfew violations listed below will be in effect. This condition is regardless of whether you live at home or live on your own. You must attend an AA, HA or NA meeting at least 5 times *per week. This does not include your agreed-upon support group, as this is more of a social gathering.*

If you obtain employment we will discuss and determine a revised curfew and out-of-bed time that fits with your work schedule.

You must be drug and alcohol free. We will provide a random test starting the week of December 19. If you refuse to take the test or fail the test, the consequences below will be in effect.

By January 1, you need to have a plan in place for moving into your own place, whether that is your own apartment or a sober living home. You should be putting enough money aside for your first month's expenses. Your plan might include a roommate, but cannot be a presently drug-using friend.

Develop 5 new friendships doing fun recreational activities with sober friends on a weekly basis, developing spiritual practices (i.e., church, Bible studies, morning devotions, support group, etc.) and getting used to honesty, accountability, discipline and responsible living.

Consequences:
If you do not meet the curfew or out-of-bed time:
First occurrence, you get one warning.
If you have a second violation, you will have to provide your own transportation to work for one week.
If you have a third violation, you will need to find a place to stay for one week outside our home.
If you have a fourth curfew violation, you will need to find a place to stay outside our home for one month.
After this if you violate the curfew, you will not be allowed to

stay in our home.

Failing or refusing to take the drug test:

First violation, you will be asked to leave the home for one month.

Second violation, you will not be allowed to live in our home.

Failing to go to AA, HA, or NA 5 times per week:

First failed week, you will have to provide your own transportation to work for one week.

Second failed week, you will have to find somewhere else to stay for one week.

Third failed week, you will no longer live in our home.

Additional Conditions:

Whether you choose to go to school or not, the following will apply:

We are no longer an ATM for you. You must be responsible for your own financial needs.

On February 1, we will no longer pay for your car insurance. You may pay us for the cost to stay on our plan for up to 6 months, due on the 15th of the month. This cost is $63 per month. After 6 months, on August 1, we will no longer pay for your insurance and you will need your own plan. If you are late for a payment we will give you one warning, the second late payment we will remove you from our insurance after 30 days.

Starting January 15th, we will no longer pay for your phone expense. You may choose to pay us $50 per month (due on the 15th) to stay on our plan. First bill is due January 15. After one warning, if you do not make the payment on time, *we will cancel the remainder of your service contract and you will be responsible for the cancelation fee due by the 15th of the following month.*

By March 1, you will need to be moved into your own place and be responsible for all your living expenses whether your own apartment or a sober living home.

We do not want this to sound harsh or in any way mean-spirited. We have spent considerable time learning how we could best help you become independent, and we believe that this is in your best interests. We want to commit to you that we will follow through with our end of this agreement in addition to unconditionally loving you as our son. If you have an issue or problem with us, our door is open to you. We can sit down and talk about it like reasonable adults, and we will talk things through with you until we figure out a solution. We will never stop caring about you, and we pray that you will take advantage of the benefits of this agreement and not focus on the consequences.

In this plan, the section on "Conditions" and the section on "Additional Conditions" are overly complex. This makes the agreed-upon conditions more difficult to monitor and also invites an abundance of arguments about compliance. So rule number one for an aftercare plan is *simplicity.*

The second major problem with this example is the consequences. They are also multilayered and too complex. There hould be only one, or two at most, levels of consequences. Rule number two is *ease of interpretation and enforcement of consequences.*

Life Balance

As complicated as our lives become, it is challenging for anyone to "keep all the balls in the air" successfully.

Life balance refers to the notion that a person is living in such a way that all of his or her different needs are being met.

Work Life: Each person has a need to use his or her gifts to contribute to society and receive financial reward for doing so. This area of life can be more or less about competition.

Love/Family Life: Most have a desire and need to grow up, fall in love, and have a spouse or significant other in his or her life. We call this love life. Also, each person has a childhood history and on-going relationship with their family of origin. Both love life and family life are more about caring and compromise.

Recreation Life: This area of a person's life addresses the human need to have a time for having fun. True recreation is the experience of doing something enjoyable where the outcome is not as important as the experience itself. In other words, true recreation is being more in the moment and enjoying what you're doing as opposed to having to accomplish some outcome. Competitive sports are an example in which the need to win can overshadow the pure enjoyment and make what was recreation more like work.

Our society does not seem to value recreation as much as we value work and love/family. Unfortunately, this causes a problem that most do not recognize. From an emotional standpoint, recreation is just as important as love/family life and work life. Just because our society does not see it that way does not make it so.

It's important to note that life balance does not mean that we spend an equal amount of time each week in each of these three areas of our life. It also does not mean that working longer hours can make up for the benefits we miss by not taking any time for recreation.

Self-improvement Life: This fourth area of life is wide-ranging. Anything you do that helps you improve yourself physically, mentally, emotionally, or spiritually is part of your self-improvement life. So this part of life might include going to the gym, working out, taking yoga, reading a self-help book, physical exercise, taking a class in school, going to see a counselor, going to a 12-step program, going to church, etc.

It can be argued that the first three areas of life (work, love/family, and recreation) provide the means to satisfy our human needs: Work, love and play. The fourth area of life, self-improvement, provides the means to develop balance in the other three.

Learning about life balance is necessary, because it could be very easy to just focus on one area of life. If the subject of life balance interests you, you might enjoy books by Abraham Maslow, who developed the Hierarchy of Human Needs theory.

In other words, living an unbalanced life is simple and easy and can come naturally. Living a balanced life requires self-awareness, the willingness to learn and change, and much work and effort.

You might notice that our society seems to have many workaholics, codependents (people overly devoted to lovers and family members), and people who just want to play all the time. Learning how to have a balanced life can be one of the most important but challenging endeavors for a human being to embark upon.

I believe that one reason alcoholics and addicts continue in their addiction is because they have an unbalanced life, which can escape attention in our culture. They are using drugs and alcohol as a substitute for something missing in their life.

Am I saying that if an addict is not working and just playing all the time, by finding employment it would get him or her off drugs or alcohol? No, it's not that simple, but it is often an important piece of the puzzle.

Would it also hold true that a man who works seventy hours a week and drinks too much, might not realize that his lack of life balance is contributing to the practicing of his addiction? My answer is, in the long-term, absolutely "yes."

While I'm not saying it's the major issue in addiction, I do believe that life balance is a key to an addict being able to have a life that he or she enjoys so much that it isn't thrown away over the immediate pleasure or relief that drugs or alcohol can provide.

Being Teachable
Teachable is another word for being humble. Is your son or daughter demonstrating an attitude of humility, which is a word used quite often in 12-step programs? How teachable, or willing to be guided, is he or she? This is an important point you can note, but not be able to do much about.

Ideally we want the person to say, "My best thinking got me here, stuck in my addiction, so I need to listen to suggestions from professionals and people in 12-step programs."

You may not, however, see that attitude in your son or daughter. It might be helpful to rate your opinion as to how teachable he or she is at various times. You could consider zero as being not very teachable, or not very willing to do things he or she doesn't like to do. A rating of ten might indicate he or she has totally surrendered to the program and is 100 percent willing to do what is suggested even if he or she doesn't like it.

So your son or daughter might, at any given time, fluctuate between zero and ten on the **teachable scale**. Obviously, you would love him or her to be a ten all the time, but that is not realistic. As he or she progresses in recovery, paying attention to your loved one's teachable scale through time a can be a helpful measure of progress.

Letting Go

Perhaps the most important thing that you can do as the parent of a recovering person, however, is let him or her go.

Ironically, letting go is tough when situations are going well. It's even harder to let go when situations provoke anxiety and worry. Such is the case when people are leaving the safe and secure confines of inpatient treatment. Parents can expect to be concerned about all of the challenges facing a loved one who is just getting out of treatment for addiction and who now must deal with all the stresses of life without the safe cocoon of the rehab environment to help them.

This is a time for parents to practice giving up control while still maintaining boundaries and consequences with their recovering sons or daughters.

Monica's Story

I received this letter in December 2012.

> *What do I do? As a mom I continue to fight this battle but I am always losing. The only thing I want is to save my son. His Junior Year, James ended up in the ER with Alcohol poisoning. He had blacked out at a party and was taken to the hospital by his friends. James was a loner, whose only purpose in life was, seemingly, to get stoned. He had lost so much at an early age and sold everything that was precious to him. The cycle continued on, and I felt like I couldn't breathe. I was drowning as much as he was and didn't know*

164

what to do. James continued to manipulate us in his senior year barely graduating.

Finally I gave him an ultimatum to get help or we would not support him at college. So he agreed and went to IOP, only to find out one week into his treatment he was arrested for a DUI with heroin and spent the night in jail. Again, we gave him another chance to go back and try to sort himself out in treatment. And, we wanted to believe him and allowed him the opportunity to go to college in August 2010.

Surprise, surprise, come November, we realized he was back using heroin — or did he ever stop? My husband and I withdrew him from school as that was our plan if he relapsed. We gave him the chance to go to sober living so he could continue with his education. But he chose to live with his girlfriend; someone who was also an addict, and we lost touch with him for six months.

In June 2011, he asked to come home as he no longer had a place to stay. Against my better judgment, we allowed it. That was a big mistake. By the second week, there were obvious signs of his drug use. He then moved out and moved into to an apartment with another junkie in a very dangerous neighborhood.

The weekend of September 26th, James came over to our house for his brother's birthday. He was beyond recognition. He was skin and bones, hair scraggy, head hung down. Even though I was his mother, he was unrecognizable to me. It just broke my heart into pieces.

On that night the last thing I said to him was, "I love you, and when you are ready for help, we are here." That's something

I said numerous times. Something else that I have never said was, "You no longer need to have that monkey on your back."

A week later, I received a text from him, "Mom I want to be me again." I jumped on that and got him into another treatment facility and was thrilled beyond words.

After two weeks, yet again, he and his girlfriend planned an escape, leaving the treatment place, and I received a call after visiting hours that James had run. In the middle of the night he called me and said, "Mom, I had a very bad night. I have been walking the streets for hours and want to get help this time."

His girlfriend had overdosed. At 5am I got in my car and took him back to the treatment center, but they would not take him back because of their policies. I sat on the curb in tears, begging them to take him, but they couldn't.

I brought him home only briefly, just enough time to call a few places and got him a bed in a couple of hours and we were on our way to Tucson. That was the beginning of a 7 month period of sobriety. Life was so good seeing the son whom you knew was hiding behind all the drugs and my life went on.

In May 2012 we received another call from his sober living place to say he hadn't returned home. My heart stopped beating. I panicked. He returned later the next day, packed up his stuff, and left his sober living house. We didn't hear from him for days until his money ran out and he needed a place to stay. He called and refused our options. He began to live on the streets of LA, and till this day, I don't know where he is living.

If I could say one thing that I have learned on this very difficult journey, is that I cannot save my son. His desire and will to want to succeed at his recovery is the key.

What I can do is save myself, learn to live life, breathe, and enjoy the things I have missed out on these last six years. And while I heal, I pray that James can heal, too. This is a real waiting game and a test of strength. I have to let go and leave it up to God.

Here is a poem about letting go. Notice how all-encompassing it is:

Letting Go

To let go does not mean to stop caring,
it means I can't do it for someone else.

To let go is not to cut myself off,
it's the realization I can't control another.

To let go is not to enable,
but allow learning from natural consequences.

To let go is to admit powerlessness, which means
the outcome is not in my hands.

To let go is not to try to change or blame another,
it's to make the most of myself

To let go is not to care for,
but to care about.

To let go is not to fix,
but to be supportive.

To let go is not to judge,
but to allow another to be a human being.

To let go is not to be in the middle arranging all the outcomes,
but to allow others to affect their destinies.

To let go is not to be protective,
it's to permit another to face reality.

To let go is not to deny,
but to accept.

To let go is not to nag, scold or argue,
but instead to search out my own shortcomings and correct them.

To let go is not to adjust everything to my desires,
but to take each day as it comes and cherish myself in it.

To let go is not to criticize or regulate anybody,
but to try to become what I dream I can be.

To let go is not to regret the past,
but to grow and live for the future.

To let go is to fear less and love more.

-Author unknown

FALL

"The foliage has been losing its freshness through the month of August, and here and there a yellow leaf shows itself like the first gray hair amidst the locks of a beauty who has seen one season too many."
—Oliver Wendell Holmes

Fall is that time on your journey when your adult child relapses. Yes, your son or daughter has had a period of progress, but he or she has returned to drugs or alcohol, and it feels as if the chill of winter has returned as the leaves fall from the trees again. Summer may be short or long, but fall can arrive unexpectedly. As unpleasant as your worry, anger, and shame may be, this turn of events is not unexpected. In fact, this emotional pain is the price we pay for caring. And winter, as we will see, has not returned ...

Relapse
As unpleasant as it is initially, relapse can be an important learning experience for your adult child and you. If it occurs, and it frequently does, focus on what you can learn from this experience. That way, your pain will have purpose and not be wasted.

A simple definition of relapse is *"A return to using an addictive substance by an addict after a period of self-imposed abstinence."* There's a saying in the recovery field that "relapse is part of recovery."

169

It is possible, however, for a person to have a successful recovery without having a single relapse. It can happen; it just doesn't happen very often. The important point here is that having a relapse is not necessary for having a successful recovery.

Nonetheless, relapse is for many people, part of recovery. Like most wise sayings, this can be easily misunderstood. When an addict hears that relapse is part of recovery, he might then say to himself, "Hey, I am going to go drink or use drugs now because relapse is part of recovery, so why not?" Yes, addicts can misuse this statement. But truth be told, they can turn around any statement and use it to justify using addictive substances.

When I hear addicts imply it is okay to relapse because of that saying, I remind them, "Yes, relapse is part of recovery, but the consequences of relapse are part of recovery, as well."

Some people have had the experience of their loved one having multiple relapses. This means that their adult child also has had multiple times of being clean and sober.

Other families will have a different experience. It might be that their adult child has never had a period of wanting to live life clean and sober, in other words, a period of self-imposed abstinence. In any case, relapse is a very common phenomenon in recovery and we want to make sure that it is not a wasted situation in which nothing was learned from the experience.

Why wasn't anything learned? Your addict adult child may not want to learn from the experience, or not believe there is anything to learn, or be too embarrassed to discuss it. These are just some of the possibilities.

The question is, will *you* learn something from it?

When your adult child relapses, you could benefit from professional help. You may not know about the relapse immediately, but as soon as you do, it is recommended you get help as soon as possible. Waiting doesn't help, and probably delays getting back on the right track.

Relapse Triggers

We talked about triggers in the previous chapter. Trigger is a word you will hear quite often in the language of recovery. We can also use the more complete term: **relapse triggers**. A relapse trigger is merely a **temptation** that comes from being reminded about something from your past.

Using the word "trigger" can be overly complicated. We could just use the word "temptation", which is much simpler and easier to understand.

A temptation relies on memory and emotion. The more intense the emotion associated with the memory, the stronger the temptation to relapse. For example, if an alcoholic sees an ad for his or her brand of beer, or is in a situation where, in the past, he or she consumed it, this can make for an intense temptation.

We mentioned the beer commercial for the alcoholic. The sight of baby powder might similarly tempt a cocaine addict.

The desire to use can come from a painful reminder as well as a pleasurable one. Painful triggers (such as feeling bored, losing a job, being angry, etc.) can all be temptations to relapse. Addicts use drugs and alcohol as a coping mechanism for dealing with life's ups and downs as well as the desire to *party, celebrate, have a good time,* etc. Addicts can be tempted by an endless variety of events in their lives.

Here are some common signs of a potential relapse. When a recovering alcoholic or addict is feeling a temptation to drink or use, **he or she might start to:**

1. isolate.
2. avoid having fun.
3. be irritated with friends or family.
4. be easily angered.
5. blame people, places, things, and conditions for his or her problems.
6. eat irregularly (over-eating, under-eating, snacking, etc.).
7. sleep irregularly (over-sleeping, under-sleeping, etc.).
8. develop an "I don't care" attitude.
9. openly reject help.
10. skip his or her twelve-step meetings.
11. develop aches and pains.
12. increase his or her use of aspirin or other non-prescription medications.
13. visit old friends and places associated with his or her addiction.
14. lose his or her normal daily routine.
15. be preoccupied with *one* area of his or her life.
16. try to force sobriety upon others.
17. avoid talking about his or her problems and recovery.
18. behave compulsively, working too much or too little, talking incessantly or not at all, etc.
19. overreact to stressful situations.
20. daydream and *wish* for things.
21. see his or her problems as unsolvable.
22. have *lethargic* periods.
23. hoard money, sex, power, etc.
24. feel sorry for him or herself.
25. face a major life change.
26. feel lonely.
27. feel powerless and helpless.

28. see his or her *plans* beginning to fail.
29. have minor depression.
30. develop unreasonable resentments.
31. feel overwhelmed.
32. convince him or herself "I'm cured."
33. doubt his or her disease.
34. lose confidence in him or herself.
35. lie consciously.
36. fantasize about drinking/using.
37. rationalize that "drinking/using can't make life any worse than it is now."
38. use a prescribed or illegal substance that is not his or her usual drug of choice.
39. practice *controlled* drinking/using.
40. experience periods of deep depression.
41. overanalyze him or herself.
42. long for happiness but not really know what it is.
43. make unrealistic or haphazard plans.
44. live in the past or in the future instead of the "here and now."
45. experience periods of confusion.
46. believe that "not drinking/using" is all he or she needs.
47. convince him or herself that "I'll never drink/use again."
48. deny his or her worries, fears, or concerns.
49. doubt his or her ability to stay sober.
50. feel like he or she is losing control.
51. daydream about failure.
52. be defensive.
53. be impatient.
54. feel exhausted.
55. expect too much from others.
56. feel disappointed.
57. get bored.

Why Relapse Happens

There is one reason for relapse, and there are a thousand excuses and rationalizations for it. The most important point to keep in mind is that when addicts are clean and sober and want to remain clean and sober, but relapse anyway, it is because they choose to.

Many addicts will tell you that they didn't want to use or drink, and yet did it anyway. There is some truth to that statement. How many of us can say we have done things that we really didn't want to do?

This is a tricky topic, one that can easily be skimmed over with a casual agreement between two caring people. The reality is that no action takes place until a person makes a decision. Although this thought indicates blame, it also provides empowerment. In 12-step programs, you might hear someone say (about a person who has relapsed), "He's just not done using yet."

The Power of Choice

A simple definition o f **empowerment** is "having choice." Having only one choice is having no choice at all. If a person has no choice in a situation we could say he or she is powerless, or we could say, is **disempowered**.

I believe that when the addictive substance is active in an addict's brain, whether it is methamphetamines or alcohol or heroin or other drugs, *then* he or she loses the power of choice and will continue to use despite the consequences.

It is important to note that I also believe that non-addicts, unless they are unconscious, do not lose their power of choice even though their brains are being affected by the addictive substance.

In other words, drugs and alcohol tempt but do not have the power of choice over the free will that we are born with unless we have the *disease* of addiction. If that were not true, every person who drank alcohol would become an alcoholic.

Yes, I believe that addictive drugs and alcohol affect addicts and alcoholics differently from those who do not have the *disease* of addiction. This is where much confusion comes in. Here is the simple definition of **addiction** I like: "Inability to control usage."

Please remember *that my beliefs are just that, the opinions of someone who has worked with thousands of addicts and families, but it is nonetheless an opinion. There are many people in this field, with much more expertise than I have, who may disagree with me. I am not trying to change anybody's opinion about a subject as complex and challenging as addiction. I am simply stating my opinion and letting you know that I am perfectly fine with those people who have a different opinion than mine.*

It's important that you decide what is true and not true for yourself, realizing that you often come across contradictory information about this complicated subject.

An Addict Is an Addict

Jeremy was a cocaine addict I counseled when I worked for a Phoenix adult rehabilitation center. At the time, he was a thirty-year-old single man who had spent most of his adult years traveling the country, partying, and avoiding responsibility.

When he came to our six-month inpatient rehab program, he had

had enough bad experiences of incarceration to make him decide that he really wanted to change. He was a model client who did very well at the center.

He completed his treatment program with only a few minor disciplinary problems. Then Jeremy moved into a halfway house, got a job, and started getting back into society, skipping the all-important aftercare steps. He had a few relapses over the next few years and, fortunately, learned from each of them.

Eventually Jeremy met a woman, fell in love, married her, and moved to Utah. Over the ensuing years from time to time he would call and let me know how he was doing. I remember one phone call we had about seven years after he had completed treatment. Out of the blue, Jeremy called one day and announced, "Mike, I have finally learned that I cannot drink."

I was very pleased to hear that, but had to put my counselor hat on and say, "Jeremy, how many times over the years have you said, 'I can drink because I'm a cocaine addict, not an alcoholic?'" Before he could answer, I said, "Let's cut to the chase. How long has it taken you to learn that you cannot drink, in spite of your experience that it always leads you back to cocaine?" Without hesitation, he answered, "Oh, about seven years."

If an alcoholic uses pot, or an opiate addict drinks alcohol, it is still a relapse. *Recovery from addiction requires **total abstinence** from all addictive substances including certain addictive prescription drugs.* Substituting one drug for another is quite common with addicts; despite their learning about this fact.

Addict or Substance Abuser?
In our society, we don't read in the newspapers, see on television or on the Internet, stories about all of the people who abuse drugs

and alcohol yet are *not* addicted. Indeed, there is much confusion about the difference between a person being addicted to drugs or alcohol and a person who simply uses too much or abuses these substances.

Abuse happens when there are negative consequences from such overuse. Substance abusers may experience a hangover the next morning from drinking. It may even cause them to have poor job performance and eventually receive a warning from the boss. Or the person who uses too many opiate prescription painkillers might have to sleep for a whole day to make up for abusing them.

This brings up a controversial subject: can a person use heroin or meth and merely abuse it without being addicted to it? I believe the answer is yes. Why should alcohol be the only drug people can use "normally" or even abuse and not be addicted to it?

My experience has shown me that people can use addictive substances like alcohol, heroin, cocaine, methamphetamine, etc. and not be addicted to them. As I have said, this is a controversial concept, and once again I remind you that the opinions in this book are mine, based on my experience. I encourage you to see them as theory and not based on scientific evidence. I strongly suggest you do as much research as possible from a wide range of sources, I am just one.

In contrast to the substance abuser, regardless of the drug or alcohol, addicts will continue to use more and more of their drug of choice despite consequences. That's because they lose the power of choice when the substance is active in their brain.

Drug and alcohol abusers can also *use* too much. But, unlike an addict, they can eventually learn to *control their usage* due to the negative consequences they suffer; and because they are able to.

We usually don't hear much about substance abusers in the press. Their stories are usually not dramatic enough to fit the media's credo about what makes the news: "If it bleeds, it leads."

Total Abstinence

Total abstinence means the abstinence, or abstaining from, use of all mind-altering substances, prescribed or not prescribed, that are addictive. This gets tricky, because although I've said the disease of addiction is in the person, not in the drug or alcohol, we still commonly use the term "addictive" when describing substances that addicts can become addicted to.

This gets especially sticky when dealing with legal prescription drugs; some are addictive and some are not.

Technically speaking, there are two categories of prescription drugs that are available today. Common prescription drugs for depression and anxiety are mind-altering substances, but they are not typically abused and addictive. Other mind-altering substances for anxiety, ADD, and pain, however, can be abused and are commonly used by addicts and alcoholics. So it's not so simple to just say that addicts and alcoholics need only stay away from all illegal mind-altering drugs (and alcohol, of course).

It is up to the recovering person and his or her family and health-care provider to determine which prescription drugs are advisable for the addict or alcoholic.

Unfortunately, there are many legal, commonly prescribed, addictive, mind-altering substances as well as many illegal, addictive, mind-altering drugs. This concept of total abstinence is complex. Nonetheless, we have to work through the complexities, because total abstinence is required for an alcoholic or addict to have a successful life of recovery.

Because maintaining total abstinence is challenging, relapse is common, so it is wise for parents to not be surprised if a relapse does occur and to actually plan for it. In our example of the Recovering Person's Plan in the previous chapter, you will notice at the bottom of the page such planning is *built in* with a space for the consequences of relapse.

I personally believe that there can be a useful purpose for relapse. It allows addicts and alcoholics to do some reality testing. They are using drugs and alcohol to cope with the stress of day-to-day living and, until they learn how to cope with the stress in new ways, that is to say non-chemical ways, they will be tempted to go back to that old tried-and-true method of instant relief that chemicals have provided in the past.

The flip side of that coin is the person who relapses when everything is going well in his or her recovery and just wants to celebrate more, feel more alive, etc. Remember that addicts use substances to cope with stress but also to have fun, or party, as they might say. That's why it is so important for addicts to find ways to have fun, excitement and fulfillment without chemical aids. In other words, ways to attain **natural highs**.

Another way to look at relapse is: For those recovering addicts who find it difficult to learn from listening to others, they may need to experience the consequences of their actions in order to provide their new learning.

What to Do When Relapse Happens

After your initial disappointment caused by your loved one's relapse, what do you do now? Fall can be a beginning instead of an end. It can be a time for you to increase your commitment to learn even more about how you have been helping your adult son or daughter.

Because there are an infinite number of situations where relapse might happen, it's important to be prepared and have some ideas of what you can do about it.

In general, you will want your loved one to experience the negative consequences of relapse, which theoretically, can help motivate him or her not to do it again. If you have some agreed-upon consequences with your son or daughter as a result of a relapse, you simply enforce the consequences.

Many parents find this difficult to do and would like to avoid the distasteful action of enforcing consequences. One of the most important things you can do, however, is follow through on agreed-upon consequences.

For instance, a son living at home might have agreed to immediately enter a halfway house if he relapses. Such an agreed-upon consequence is not designed as punishment, it is designed to provide a less stressful environment for your loved one to learn life coping skills without having to use drugs or alcohol.

For most people, living at home is the most stressful situation they can be in. Yes, it is potentially the most comfortable, but it is also the most stressful because of all the history at home with loving, caring and sometimes controlling (out of fear) family members.

Typically, a less stressful environment, and one more conducive to learning life skills, is a halfway house. There, recovering people are surrounded by their peers to whom they can say anything without worrying about being misunderstood.

Final Financial Help
Above all, we want to make sure you are not accidentally or unintentionally funding relapse. This can be tricky, especially if you

have a history of paying out a lot of money over a long period of time trying to help your addicted son or daughter.

Yes, you worked with the Financial Strings Checklist in the Spring chapter, but in Fall, you may find that you want to revisit that checklist and address cutting final strings you might not have dealt with.

A helpful tool for this process is the **Final Financial Help Agreement.** The goal is to help your son or daughter one final time and put him or her on notice that this is the last time.

This is good for you, and it is also good for your adult child. Finally your child knows he or she is responsible for his or her own actions. While this has its frightening aspects, it also empowers your loved one to be in charge of his or her own life.

One of the additional benefits of your adult child knowing this is the last time you will be paying to help him or her is that he or she may take any help you are paying for more seriously.

This agreement is to be completed with your adult child. If you are in a relationship, it's important that you and your spouse agree on what you are willing to do financially. It's also important to know what you want and what you're willing to negotiate, based on what your loved one is asking for. At this time, having the help of a professional substance abuse counselor or recovery coach might be very helpful.

An example of a Final Financial Help Agreement with multiple choices for each section follows. These options provide food for thought for what you and your adult child might want to do in your specific situation.

At www.palgroup.org, you can find a blank version of this form that you can print and use.

Final Financial Help Agreement

Examples

Person In Need: John J. Smith

Date: Sept. 22, 2013

As your __x__ parent(s) ____ grandparent(s) ___other:
because I/we love you and want the best for you, and also because of our history of helping you financially, I/we enter into the following agreement with you:

In consideration of my (our) willingness to help you financially one last time by:

Example 1. Pay for inpatient treatment, not to exceed $9,500.

Example 2 Giving you $750 cash to use any way you choose.

Example 3. Paying off $600 truck loan and putting the title in your name only.

Example 4. Paying your attorney on your charge ARS 934012 only.

Example 5. Paying for one month at the halfway house of your choice.

Example 6. Covering your health insurance for six months until 12/31/13.

If you accept this offer, I/we ask you to agree to never ask for money or financial help of any kind ever again (except for documented medical help).

As the Person In Need and in consideration of the financial help listed above, I agree to never ask for, or expect financial help ever again (except for documented medical help).

_____   _____
Person In Need Signature   My Family/Friend Signature

Multiple Treatment Attempts

How many times have you experienced the hope of summer, then have that hope dashed by the cold harsh reality of fall? If you are parents of an adult child with a history of multiple treatment attempts and multiple relapses, you are not alone.

There may still be some things for you to learn. If you find that you are staying stuck in that hopeless feeling of winter for an extended period of time, this is most often a sign that you need some personal counseling to help you deal with all the hurtful emotions locked inside of you.

The promise made in this book is that, through your commitment to continuing education, you will eventually experience "no more winter."

Realistically speaking, it is hard *not* to go into winter when your adult child relapses (yet again!). So it is more reasonable to promise that, with your continuing education, those unplanned visits back to winter will be of shorter and shorter duration. It's one thing to visit winter for a time and quite another to find yourself *living there.*

You might ask, "How many more of these relapses must we endure?" That question is about a subject over which you have no control.

A better question is, "How long will I stay in winter?" That is something you do have some control over. The answer to that question is "You will leave winter as soon as you are ready to re-enter spring."

Notes:

NO MORE WINTER

"Winter must be cold
for those with no warm memories."
— From the movie *An Affair to Remember*

In recovery, winter was a stage of ignorance and shock of finding out your adult child had an addiction. Now the things you know, you cannot deny anymore. Through this process, your loved one also has learned things he or she cannot unlearn. So you will still have spring, you will still have summer, and you may still have fall, but you will suffer no more winters, except ideally, for the briefest of moments, because you have changed. Even if you do have those dark moments, they will be briefer and briefer. Their brevity is a measure of your growth.

Why There's No Going Back
We have talked about this process as a journey, and it is a journey through the seasons of life. When you have come far by learning not only what is happening but also how to change your destination, there is no going back without your consent.

There will always be more to learn, things to tweak as you and your loved one continue on your personal journey, this journey called life.

Once you're able to see the big picture of where you are heading, it doesn't mean you know everything and have all the answers. Of course, there may be more big surprises in which you do not have

185

any idea what to do. But now you have a roadmap for adjusting your journey. You either know what you need to do, or you know where to get the answers so that you may achieve your goals.

Minding Expectations

One of the things parents learn on this journey is to be more aware of and manage expectations. Expectations are a normal part of being human.

Sometimes you don't recognize your own expectations until a sense of disappointment occurs; that is one way to identify an expectation you may not even have known you had.

The higher the expectation, the more severe your disappointment. When an upsetting situation occurs with your adult child, such as relapse, you will naturally be disappointed. If you are surprised how disappointed you are, however, that may well be a sign that your expectations might have been higher than you even knew. Your extreme level of disappointment is your responsibility to manage.

M.Y.E.

This is an acronym reminding you to Mind Your Expectations. It is commonly heard in PAL meetings, especially when parents are enthusiastically talking about how well their sons or daughters are doing in recovery. The intention of MYE is not to be negative, but rather to be realistically positive in order to avoid severe, debilitating disappointment.

Being more aware of your expectations and taking the responsibility to manage them is a very important habit to cultivate. We are not suggesting that you have no expectations at all, because that is not possible. But by making a commitment to being more vigilant and more aware of your thoughts, you can learn to limit your expectations. It is when our expectations are *flights of fancy* that we suffer the most severe disappointment. In fact, members of Alcoholics Anonymous' often refer to expectations as *future resentments*.

There are many opportunities on this journey to rationalize situations and believe that your expectations are reasonable. We need to be open-minded to the fact, however, that no one is an expert on reasonability. Managing your expectations by taking responsibility for noticing them and adjusting them (downward, in most cases) will help not only you, but will also help your addicted loved one. Your entire family will also probably benefit.

The Hope Hotel
This is a helpful metaphor for this invisible process of minding your expectations in your thoughts.

When your child is doing well, you may find yourself on the twentieth floor of the Hope Hotel. Some of you may even find yourself on the 200th floor.

The higher you are because your child is doing so well, the farther you will fall when your child is not doing so well.

You have no control over whether your child relapses or not. You do have control, however, over how high your expectations are. Most parents have to practice noticing which floor of the Hope Hotel they find themselves on, and then get on the elevator and go back down to the second floor. After all, it hurts much less to fall two floors than it does to fall twenty or 200.

Use Your Support Team
Because of your educational journey, now you have a team. Your team consists of fellow self-help group members, counselors, coaches, etc. You put it together, and it's still in place. If you are in contact with your adult child, and he or she is not in recovery, you are

still praying for him or her and helping as best you can in a healthy, limited, precise way.

You are putting into practice what you have learned more and more as time goes on. You are spending less mental energy on your suffering adult child and getting on with your own life in as healthy a way as you can. Now you are not your son or daughter's life coach any more, now you are his or her *role model.*

It may have taken you a while to get to this point in life, but it will feel like the journey has not been wasted. You remind yourself that you are in a much better position to help your loved one when he or she is ready.

You are a much healthier person to be around, and that benefits the other members of your family, too. You have not forgotten or forsaken your suffering loved one; you are merely being more patient and willing to let a higher power guide his or her recovery process instead of you trying to force him or her to change. Reminders from twelve-step programs such as "One day at a time," "God is in charge, and I am okay," and "Easy does it" are truly helpful.

Nuggets: Helpful Sayings for Parents
Here are some helpful sayings that we use in PAL groups for parents to keep in mind and use as affirmations over the long haul. We call them Nuggets. You can also find them on the PAL Web site.

"People don't change when they see the light, they change when they feel the heat."

"This is a marathon, not a sprint."

"The faintest ink is better than the best memory."
(This refers to the importance of putting contracts and agreements in writing.)

"Baby steps"

"Sometimes it's best to just listen and say nothing."

"Resilience comes from coping with adversity."

"This, too, shall pass."

"I'm picking my battles."

"I'm getting comfortable with silence."

"Parents can give their children everything but common sense."

"When it comes to our children, every parent is blind."
— *Yiddish saying*

"If you don't do the work, you don't get better."
— *AA saying*

"Short-term pain for long-term gain."
— *AA saying*

"I'm learning to bite my tongue."
— *PAL mom*

"The answer to the mystery is always in the history."

"Words are weak adversaries of drugs."
— *William L. Fountain*

"To a teenager, the word 'no' is an aphrodisiac."

"Desperation is the prelude to surrender."
— *Marushka*

"If nothing changes, nothing changes."
— *AA saying*

"I need to stop trying to *choreograph* his recovery."

When You're Not in Touch

If you are in the situation of having a child who is not in recovery and not in touch with you, we call this stage the **prodigal son time**. You are moving forward in your life, but not forgetting your son or daughter, who is hurting. You are learning how to make peace with the fact that you are not able to have regular contact with him or her. You have learned how to have more meaning in your own life from other people, family members, and other interests.

A good example of this is Jackie. She had been attending PAL Group meetings for about nine months when she came into a meeting and shared something important with us. "I still have had no contact with my son, who has been living out of state," she said. "It's been over three years, but I'm sleeping at night now for the first time in a long time. I've come to know a new peace, even though I'm not in contact with my son."

When other parents asked her, "How is that possible?" she answered, "Through what I've learned in these meetings and my faith in God."

Because some parents still looked puzzled, I added, "In my experience, education leads to understanding, understanding can lead to acceptance of things I do not have the power to change, and acceptance leads to peace." Acceptance does not mean something is right or good. It means I may not be able to change it no matter how bad I feel about it.

Even though being at peace and not in pain may look selfish to those who are uneducated about such things, you have realized that keeping yourself healthy and moving forward in your life is one of the best things you can do for your child and the rest of your family.

How Can I Know When I've Done All I Can Do?

I am frequently asked by parents, "How can I know I've done all I can do?" This question may indicate they still think they are in control over whether their son or daughter gets sober. They may fear that, if they don't do everything they can, they are failures as parents.

To think you have that power only leads to hopelessness and despair. After reading this book, hopefully they can put their misplaced guilt and shame about this issue behind them, and be more at peace.

Or perhaps your loved one has demonstrated successful long-term recovery in their time and their way. This is truly a great feeling.

Either way, because of the time and effort you have put into your education, a time comes when you realize you have crossed into a new, more peaceful way of living. It may surprise you, but suddenly you realize you are doing the best you can do for your adult child and for yourself. No matter where your addicted loved one is in his or her own life, you are certainly in a better place to help both your adult child and yourself.

At this point, congratulate yourself, knowing that you have achieved a peace that you have earned through your commitment and often heart-wrenching efforts.

Magic Moment No. 6: You Are Experiencing a New Level of Peace:

You are feeling greater serenity because you know in your heart that your hard work has paid off and that you are doing the very best you can for yourself and your loved one.

Janel Today

Janel has experienced Magic Moment #6: Peace. As of this printing, Ernie has been clean and sober for six years. He has a job helping addicts and their families, he has healthy hobbies and healthy friends, and Janel sees her son as a healthy adult man.

Janel is not alone. She and thousands of other parents have experienced their children's successful recovery from alcohol and drugs.

Like you, the successful parents' journeys started in a cold, dark winter they did not expect. Also like them, you and your family can live a healthy, happy life.

ADDITIONAL RESOURCES

Fortunately, there are abundant resources available to help you through the seasons of recovery, and the number of resources continues to increase. You can find them from professionals in the recovery field, in books, online, and in support groups.

Here are some I consider valuable to have at your fingertips. I hope you find them helpful, too.

WHAT DO I DO WHEN...

This section provides you with specific options and choices when facing certain predictable issues on the long journey of recovery.

The following options and choices are some possible helpful ways to react to common problems. They may or may not work for you, but they are solutions and approaches that have worked for others.

Please remember: do not construe the following as advice. I always recommend that you seek professional help, and let professionals help guide you and give you the advice you need as each situation may have its own issues.

IN EVERY SITUATION...

Take a deep breath.

With all the brain imaging technology of today, it is a well-documented fact that your stress level can affect your ability to think clearly, think logically, and access important memory. We could restate that thought as "When my stress level gets too high, it can make my thinking unclear, illogical, and without the benefit of past knowledge previously gained." Therefore, keeping your stress level down helps you in many ways.

There is usually a consistent onslaught of drama and trauma in addict's lives. With your commitment to helping your child, these twin disruptions to your serenity will invade your life as well.

With this in mind, it just makes good sense to sit down, take a deep breath, and notice what's going on in your mind.

Before you take action, it can be helpful for you to ask yourself in each situation:

"Is this a minor inconvenience, a major inconvenience, or a real catastrophe?"

This allows you to assess the importance of each situation before proceeding as you also take some deep breaths.

Follow the two Cardinal Rules.
No matter what the situation is, when your adult child is in need of help, it's helpful to remember these two Cardinal Rules:

No unasked-for help
You may have trained your loved one to merely complain ("I'm hungry, cold, broke,") etc. and then you jump in and offer help he or she has not even asked for. This deprives your adult child of ownership and responsibility for the solution. So they learn nothing from the situation, and nothing changes. As adults, people need to be responsible for asking clearly for what they want.

No instant answers
Requiring an instant answer often pressures you into not making

the best decision in the moment. Delaying the answer, except in life-threatening situations, gives you time to consult with others and think the request through. It also provides perspective for your loved one, who may have developed the habit of turning every little problem into a major drama. It can be helpful to simply say, "I'll have to get back to you."

Once your loved one knows that his or her drama (often used to get you to act so quickly you don't have time to think) cannot draw you away from the two Cardinal Rules, now you both can have a more productive conversation.

SPECIFIC SITUATIONS

What do I do when my adult child relapses?
This is a very common occurrence and there are many factors to take into account because of all the variables in each individual's life history. The most important thing is to make sure that there are consequences associated with the relapse. That's not something you will always have some control over, but it's important to know that consequences are necessary for your adult child to learn something from the experience that will help him or her in the future.

When your child is living in your home, you are in an excellent position to impose consequences for a relapse. A common, helpful consequence of relapse is to have him or her move into some form of sober living. This is not punishment. Rather, relapse can be seen as "asking for help" to move into a living situation where he or she has more constant support from recovering people. This is what sober living provides.

If your child is living on his or her own but still requires financial support, such as for housing or school, you are still in a good position to impose consequences. One young man I worked with

195

had completed rehab, was living in a halfway house, had a job, and owned his own car.

When he relapsed, the people running the halfway house asked him to leave for three days and offered him the opportunity to come back after that time. He showed up at his parents' house, asking to stay there for those three days. His parents did not want to reward his relapse by letting him come home. So, they said "no". He slept in his car for three days and then went back to the halfway house. That was a helpful consequence.

Even if you are dealing with a totally independent son or daughter, you can still help by not saving him or her from the consequences of the relapse and by not rewarding his or her actions. For instance, if your adult child relapsed and got a DUI and had to pay a big fine, he or she now has to pay that fine. In the past you might have jumped in to help. In this situation, your refusal to help can be a gift to your son or daughter by helping him or her accept more of the responsibility of adulthood.

What do I do when my son or daughter calls and needs to be rescued right now?
Stay calm. Find out if he or she is in any immediate danger. If so, this is the time to ask for help and call on professionals, whether it is police, a crisis unit, ambulance, etc.

If he or she is not in immediate danger, ask yourself if you are helping your adult child with an everyday living issue or with his or her recovery. If your loved one is serious about wanting recovery help at this time, you can contact appropriate recovery professionals. If all he or she wants is help to continue living in an addictive lifestyle, however, remember the Two Cardinal Rules: "No unasked for help," and "No instant answers."

What do I do if my loved one accuses me of not loving him or her anymore?

If your adult child says, "But I thought you loved me," an easy response is, "Pack your bags, we're going on a guilt trip." By saying this, you are "calling" your adult child on his or her emotional blackmail. In fact, by making him or her face up to his or her own responsibility, you are truly showing your love.

Whenever you are accused of not loving your adult child anymore, whether it's from that child or someone else, it is a good time to revisit the "Big Five Ways to Show Love" in the Spring chapter.

What do I do when my son or daughter commits to a goal, but does not follow through?

If the Goal Involves You

Confront your son or daughter and have a straight talk about the situation. This could be a very helpful opportunity to practice talking to your adult child as an adult even if he or she is acting like a child.

If the follow-through never happens, then you can set a consequence, and follow through on that consequence.

For example, if your loved one committed to getting your car washed and does not follow through, ask him or her to agree to a target date for getting the car washed, then further agree if he or she does not do it by that date, you will not allow him or her to use the car for a week.

If the Goal Does Not Involve You

Perhaps your son or daughter has committed to signing up for school by a certain date and doesn't follow through. This could be an opportunity for you to treat him or her as an adult and maintain the attitude of "It's your life, and if you want to go to school, you go to school, and if you don't you won't. It's all up to you." Once again, it provides a teachable moment, an opportunity for you to treat your adult child like an adult. It may not be easy, but it can be invaluable.

What do I do when I discover that my adult child has been using heroin?

Heroin use in the United States is soaring, especially in rural areas, as the supply is increasingly easy to get and as other drugs and alcohol become more costly. The number of people who say they have used heroin in the past year jumped 53.5% between 2002 to 2011, according to the Substance Abuse and Mental Health Services Administration. In 2010, there was a 55% increase of overdoses from 2000, according to the Centers for Disease Control and Prevention.

The simple answer is to get professional help as soon as possible. You can call a treatment center, a substance abuse counselor, and even a professional interventionist in your area. There also are support groups such as PAL, Al-anon, and Nar-anon.

Getting help from professionals will be the fastest, easiest, and best solution to the many questions that are racing through your mind. When looking for counselors, ask for a referral from a local substance abuse treatment center or fellow members of a self-help group.

You can also check the Internet for professionals in your area by searching for your city or state and the words "substance abuse counselor." For example, you could search for "Omaha substance abuse counselor."

What do I do when my adult child drops his or her baby off at our house?

This is a challenging situation. If your addict child is not in recovery, you don't want to enable him or her. You also don't want your grandchild to suffer needlessly. In most situations I have worked with, the addict will use the baby to manipulate the parents to get money for drugs or alcohol.

Before this situation ever occurs, you can make it clear to your son or daughter what you and your spouse's position is on this matter. The two of you must agree wholeheartedly and be ready with what actions you plan to take (requesting custody, referring him or her to someone who will watch the baby, etc.).

This is a time to get professional help from a substance abuse counselor and also information from parents who can share their similar experiences. We have PAL facilitators in the Phoenix area who are grandparents of an addict, and who have experienced resolution. They are happy to share their experiences with grandparents who are in the midst of this challenging problem.

What do I do when I have not heard a word from my addicted loved one in weeks?
It is helpful to decide whether you feel worse when you have no contact with your adult child, or worse when you are involved in his or her day-to-day drama and upsetting life details. This knowledge can help you either accept not hearing from him or her, or accept the drama and trauma of being in touch. This is a difficult topic you may want to explore with professional help.

If you have decided that you are better off not hearing, yet start to feel heartsick when you don't, remember that you have made a choice. Remind yourself that you made this choice, and why you made it. Each time, you will feel a little better about not hearing from your adult child.

If you have decided to accept the drama and trauma so that you may stay in touch, take a moment to think about your purpose for contact.

Do you just want to find out that he or she is okay? Do you want to ask him or her one more time to get help? Do you want to offer to help your child yourself? These are all important questions that focus on you, but the answers to these questions will be important to him or her.

If you decide to make contact and if you know where he or she is living, you can just drop by. If you don't know where your loved one is but he or she has a cell phone, you could call or text. Or, if he or she has e-mail, you could make contact that way.

If you can contact your loved one, it's always okay to send this message orally, electronically, or even in writing: "I love you, and I always will. Please let me know if I can ever be of help to you." Keep in mind that you are telling your adult child that it is okay to ask. This is not a commitment to comply with their request.

What do I do when my ex-spouse is enabling my adult child?
Honest and open communication is the best approach with your ex-spouse, and perhaps seeing a substance abuse counselor or coach might help negotiate some agreement about the best way to help.

If he or she is enabling your adult child, have a conversation in which you clearly and calmly speak without talking down to him or her.

What do I do when my son or daughter comes home after completing rehab?
As we discussed in detail in the book, an aftercare plan is critical. It is your and your adult child's framework for the future. That plan should be something that is constantly referred to and discussed.

What do I do when my adult child is diagnosed as bipolar?
Some substance abuse professionals estimate that as many as 50% of all addicts are bipolar. In fact, some professionals theorize that drugs and alcohol are used to medicate the bipolar disorder. In any

event, having a good, solid diagnosis with a skilled psychiatrist *who also knows about addiction* is the best approach.

An addict needs to be clean and sober for at least two weeks or sometimes longer in order to get an accurate diagnosis. With a proper diagnosis and prescribed medication, most people suffering from bipolar disorder can be helped. A professional should help your adult child with medication and compliance.

What do I do if my son or daughter is threatening suicide?
This is clearly a very serious matter. If there is a threat, do not delay in making use of all the resources at your command.

If a suicide threat has been made before, it is good to be prepared should your adult child threaten this action again. I highly recommend you have the contact information for any helpful resources for suicide available should you ever need them.

In some communities, a mobile crisis unit for behavioral health issues is available, and the police can also be helpful at this time. Crisis hotlines are another good source of assistance.

What do I do when my son or daughter has been in rehab multiple times and still continues to relapse?
At this point, your adult child may be considered **treatment-wise**. That means he or she has been in treatment enough times to be able to *teach* recovery. That does not however, mean your loved one has learned about it. It only means he or she is probably a good talker and as they say in AA, "It's easy to talk the talk, but you have to walk the walk."

If your adult child is asking for help for his or her drug or alcohol problem, this is a good time to get a professional involved.

If your loved one says, "I want to go to treatment one more time" and you have the financial ability and willingness, you could use the Final Financial Help Agreement in the No More Winter chapter of this book.

Another choice is to say to your adult child, "We've already helped you X number of times, and now it's up to you to find your own help." Or, you might say, "This journey with you has been way too long and way too upsetting for us. We still love you, and we do believe that you will get help someday for your problems. It's just too painful for us, though, to be involved in the details of such help. Please do not contact us, unless it's a life or death emergency, or until you have at least six months of documented recovery."

Again, it is helpful to have thought through how you will handle this situation in advance should it occur.

What do I do to help my adult child deal with a big disappointment he or she is facing?
First, notice how concerned you are about your child dealing with a big disappointment and take a moment to figure out why you feel that way.

Are you worried that the disappointment might cause your son or daughter to relapse? If so, it could be very helpful for you to confront him or her in a caring way and communicate your concerns. Another option is to say to your adult child, "Please let me know if I can help you deal with this."

In both cases, you're treating your loved one like an adult, discussing it rather than thinking for him or her and predicting the future possibilities because of a disappointment.

What do I do when my son or daughter is facing incarceration?
This is a very serious problem, and there is no one simple answer

that fits every situation. If your loved one is facing long term jail or prison time it means he or she is being charged with committing a serious crime.

You need to take some time and ask yourself some important questions, including how often your adult child has been in legal trouble, how often he or she has attempted recovery, and how much time and effort you have spent helping your adult child without much progress.

There are no guarantees, of course, but it's possible that incarceration just might provide the wake-up call your loved one needs to finally get serious about recovery. Over the years I've met many men and women who have done this.

If this is your adult child's first problem with the law, it may make sense to help financially with an attorney or with bail.

If you believe your son or daughter is innocent, you may find yourself doing everything in your power to help.

This would certainly be a good time to talk to other parents who have been through this as well as an experienced substance abuse counselor.

SUGGESTED READING

These are some of the books I recommend frequently to families that I coach and to those who attend PAL Group meetings.

The Addictive Personality: Understanding the Addictive Process and Compulsive Behavior, by Craig Nakkan. Hazelden,1988

Addicted Like Me: A Mother-Daughter Story of Substance Abuse and Recovery, by Karen Franklin. Seal Press, 2009

Beautiful Boy: A Father's Journey Through His Son's Addiction, by David Sheff. Houghton Mifflin Co., 2008

Codependent No More, How to Stop Controlling Others and Start Caring for Yourself, by Melodie Beattie. Hazelden, 1986

Don't Let Your Kids Kill You: A Guide for Parents of Drug and Alcohol Addicted Children, by Charles Rubin. New Century Publishers, 2008

The Interventionist, by Joani Gammill. Hazelden, 2011

The Language of Letting Go: Daily Meditations for Co-Dependents (Hazelden Meditation Series), by Melodie Beattie. Hazelden, 1990

Mindset: The New Psychology of Success, by Carol Dweck. Random House, 2007.

On Grief and Grieving: Finding the Meaning of Grief Through the Five Stages of Loss, by Elisabeth Kubler-Ross, David Kessler. Scribner, 2005

Parent to Parent: A Daily Reader for Parents of a Child Who is Abusing Alcohol or Drugs, Meek Press, 2001

Peaceful Parent, Happy Kids: How to Stop Yelling and Start Connecting, by Dr. Laura Markham. Penguin Group, 2012

Setting Boundaries(TM) with Your Adult Children: Six Steps to Hope and Healing for Struggling Parents, by Allison Bottke. Harvest House, 2008

Smoke and Mirrors: The Magical World of Chemical Dependency, by Dorothy Marie England. Forward Movement, 1995.

Sweat: A Practical Plan For Keeping Your Heart Intact While Loving An Addict, by Denise Krochta. Dog Ear Publishing, 2011.

Tweak: Growing Up on Methamphetamines, by Nic Sheff. Simon & Schuster, 2007.

When I Lay My Isaac Down: Unshakable Faith in Unthinkable Circumstances, by Carol J Kent. NavPress, 2004.

Wild at Heart: Discovering the secret of a Man's Soul, by John Eldredge. Thomas Nelson, 2001.

HELPFUL ORGANIZATIONS
There are many organizations that can help you and your loved one. Some have chapters throughout the United States, while others are local. Here are some of them, presented in alphabetical order.

Al-Anon
www.al-anon.org
757-563-1600
wso@al-anon.org
A support group for families of problem drinkers

CoDA
www.coda.org
602- 277-7991, 888-444-2359 (toll free), 888-444-2379 (Spanish toll free)
info@ coda.org
A fellowship of men and women whose purpose is to develop healthy relationships.

Families Anonymous
www.familiesanonymous.org
847-294-5877

famanon@familiesanonymous.org
A support group for families of addicts.

Nar-Anon
www.nar-anon.org
310-534-8188, 800-477-6291 (toll free)
wso@nar-anon.org
A support group for families of addicts.

PAL Group
www.palgroup.org
info@palgroup.org
A support group of parents helping parents who have a child
suffering from addiction.

WHAT IS A PAL GROUP?
Parents of Addicted Loved ones (PAL) is a support group of parents
helping parents. PAL can also help spouses who feel the need to
parent their addicted partners. All family members and friends are
also welcome at its meetings.

There are numerous chapters in Arizona, and new ones starting
across the United States. These groups meet every week to offer
education and support, at no charge, for parents who are trying to
save a son or daughter from addiction. A list of PAL Group meeting
locations can be found at www.palgroup.org .

By attending PAL meetings, you will learn proven ways to help your
loved one recover from his or her addiction. You'll also have an
opportunity to give support to and receive support from others who
are facing the same challenges you are.

Although you may choose to attend a PAL Group near your home or office, some parents prefer to attend a group where they are not likely to encounter neighbors, friends, or co-workers.

We also have a monthly PAL meeting by phone for people who do not live near a meeting location. Information about this is also on the PAL Web site.

How to Start a PAL Group in Your Area

What if you live in an area that does not have a group to help parents? The most important element in getting started is the power of a person's desire to make it happen. With a shared goal of two or more people working together, it works even better.

If having a group is something you feel will help, anyone can start a new PAL Group by following a few simple steps, which can be found on the PAL Group Web site at www.palgroup.org .

For information about how a typical meeting is run, look at our PAL Meeting Format, PAL Group Facilitator Guidelines, and our Facilitator Resources page on the PAL Web site.

Most meetings are about one-and-a-half hours long and held on weekday evenings.

Facilitator training is conducted in Phoenix four times annually.

Keep in mind that a volunteer facilitator is not a teacher. Teachers need to have total knowledge of the subject they teach. A facilitator is more like a timekeeper, guide, and fellow student who is learning the curriculum along with the other group members.

The Web site gives you more information about whom to contact to get started. A mentor will then get in touch to guide you through the start-up process.

THE SIX MAGIC MOMENTS
These magic moments are pivotal times when you are able to make commitments to yourself and your loved one that show your progress.

They are good times for acknowledging that you have reached a milestone in your own recovery. They are a good time to feel positive about what you are doing and the growth you are experiencing.

Sometimes they also let you know where and when you are stuck. You may have one or more Magic Moments that are difficult for you to achieve. If so, working with a counselor can help you evaluate these issues.

Magic Moment #1: Committing to Recognizing the Truth and Announcing Your Discovery to Your Loved One.
This is when you tell your loved one, *"I know about your problem. I still love you and will do everything I can to get you help to resolve it."*

This marks the time when you enter winter. You make the commitment to accept an unpleasant truth. You can acknowledge to yourself that your adult child really does have a drug or alcohol problem. It's not necessarily that you were in denial before. It may be that now you see irrefutable evidence.

You and your loved one, as well as any other family members who may be involved (spouses, partners, their children, grandparents and others) are now operating from a different baseline. All of you can now proceed from this point of honesty, knowing that there is a problem and it must be dealt with.

Magic Moment #2: Committing to Getting New Learning and Letting Your Adult Child Know You Are Doing So.

This is the opportunity that goes along with entering spring. You have made the commitment to take the action steps necessary to learn about recovery from addiction with the hope that your new learning will help you help your son or daughter with his or her drug or alcohol problem. At the very least, it will help you with what you need to know and do, regarding your loved one's addiction.

This education can come from attending support groups, seeing a counselor for your own issues, reading books, etc. You are able to say to your adult child, *"I'm educating myself in order to help you better."*

Making this decision, and letting your loved one know you have made it, is an important step in changing the old pattern of helping your adult child. This does not mean you are abandoning your loved one, rather it means you are doing your part to help him or her become the independent adult you want you child to be. You are going to have new knowledge that lets you interact with your adult child differently, and he or she will know this is so. You are moving ahead.

Magic Moment #3: Apologizing for Not Treating Your Adult Child Like an Adult.

This is when you admit to yourself and announce to your adult child that you have unintentionally made the mistake of treating him or her as if he or she were a child instead of an adult and are ready to apologize for having done it. You are able to say, *"We love you very much, and thought we were helping by treating you like a child. Now we realize that you deserve to be treated like the adult you are."*

This moment allows you and your adult child to acknowledge an unintended mistake. Something for which you do not need to continue suffering false guilt over. Now you can move on from it.

Magic Moment #4: Committing to Changing How You Help.
This is when you announce to your son or daughter that you are changing how you will help him or her in the future. It can be helpful to reveal your intention to change as not being conditional on whether they change or not. It may sound something like this: "Because of my new education, I am going to adjust the way I help you in the future. I intend to help you more like the adult you are. *"I am going to treat you like the adult you are, and adjust the way I help you accordingly."*

Magic Moment #5: Committing to Cutting Financial Strings.
This is when you commit to taking the risk of limiting and even ending certain financial aid to your son or daughter.

With your new learning about the risks of continuing to help with money, you're in a better position now to weigh the risks of helping versus the benefits of *not* helping.

This is when you reveal your intention to change how you help your son or daughter financially. "Strings" is a metaphor for the potential for manipulation that invariably accompanies financial help.

The cutting of strings is a process best completed through time and negotiation with your son or daughter. The goal is to end any potential for manipulation, either by giver or by receiver. Also, this demonstrates your belief in your adult child's ability to become an independent person.

You experience this critical Magic Moment when you tell your loved one, *"We have been inadvertently preventing you from learning financial responsibility, something every adult must know. That is not our intention, so we are going to cut the financial strings that have held you back."*

Magic Moment #6: Experiencing a New Level of Peace

There comes a time when you realize that you are feeling greater serenity because you know in your heart that your hard work has paid off, that you are doing the very best you can for yourself and your loved one.

This time does not come on command but as a result of your incremental awareness through time and awareness of the truth.

This moment is not unlike that of the relief that addicts report when they finally *accept the unacceptable* by surrendering to undesirable reality: "You can't control your loved one."

Most addicts wish and hope they could control their drinking or drug use and typically must go through many painful experiences to finally surrender to the fact that they can't. The AA *Big Book* calls it "a moment of clarity."

For you as a parent of an addicted or recovering loved one, this is your moment of clarity, one that can bestow amazing peace upon you.

Janel's Complete Story

Throughout this book, we have used the story of Janel, a PAL mom, to illustrate the various steps that most parents go though and to demonstrate the power of incremental learning.

Here we offer her story in its entirety.

Janel, a single mom and a nurse with two sons, got the shock of her life when she noticed needle marks on her nineteen-year-old son Ernie's arms. "I remember that moment and the flood of emotions that overwhelmed me," recalls Janel.

When he was younger, Ernie had behavioral problems, and Janel had done her best to help him. As a child, he was sent to wilderness camp, and when he got older, he attended boarding school.

With this revelation of Ernie's drug use, Janel realized her worst fears had been realized. She did not know it at the time, but this was to be a long journey for Ernie and her, a journey of hope and of hopes crushed.

Janel's Repetitive Winter
Although Ernie had been in rehab several times for his opiate addiction, by age twenty-six, Ernie had yet to show a consistent desire for recovery. Like so many parents with this problem, Janel had lived a roller-coaster-like life because of Ernie's erratic attempts to get help.

Each time, however, she knew that she was better off than she had been before she began educating herself. She remained consistent in how she interacted with Ernie despite his relapses.

Janel Gets Help for Herself
At this point in her story, Janel is ready to get help, but this time for herself. The first time Janel came to a family support group, she looked stressed and lost, but she was listening and open to sharing her thoughts and her true feelings. In a word, she was participating.

Janel shared with the group that she thought all she had to do was to get her son into Calvary's thirty-day rehab program and everything would be fine. He would come out after a month, and all of the problems he'd always had would be taken care of.

She laughs at herself now when talking about this, but back then that is how she truly felt. This expectation explains her deep disappointment when Ernie not only left treatment early on his own against staff advice and went back to using drugs, he also went back to the drug-using girlfriend with whom he was in a co-dependent relationship.

Janel was happy when she was able to talk Ernie into going back and completing his program at the Calvary Addiction Recovery Center. Then he left treatment early again, however, this time he was asked to leave the center for severe misconduct. And once again, he returned to the drugs and the girlfriend.

Janel reported that she was tired of the roller-coaster ride of feeling great when Ernie was getting help and then deeply depressed when he relapsed.

As a healthcare professional herself, she smiled when she said, "I think I've become bipolar because of my son!" Finally, Janel was ready to learn how to help Ernie without enabling him.

She did not know it at the time, but she soon discovered that she could accomplish that goal. Sure, it would take time, but not an unreasonable amount of it. More importantly, she learned that it *was* possible, and she wanted to do it. This was the beginning of her discovery of hope.

Janel Takes a Risk

By this time in Janel's journey, Janel's son Ernie had been in and out of rehab several times for his opiate addiction, and even though he was twenty-six, he had never shown a consistent desire for recovery. Ernie had recently been asked to leave rehab for using heroin on the premises and was back living with a girlfriend who was also a drug addict. This was a major heartache for Janel as she continued to try to help him with his drug problem.

By the time Janel attended her first PAL meeting, she reported that

Ernie was now living on the streets with a friend, and both of them were using heroin. She said she would often drive down to the area Ernie lived in, find him, and give him food. She also allowed Ernie to show up at her home at any time, come in, and take a shower. She was a loving mom and wanted to help her son.

As Janel began to learn the difference between enabling and healthy helping, she made some changes. After about two months of coming to PAL meetings, Janel reported that she called her son on his cell phone and told him that she would no longer be bringing food to him on the street. He responded, "Whatever."

She was obviously nervous about not feeding Ernie and worried about what would happen to him if she stopped her loving deliveries. Although this was never discussed, from an emotional standpoint, I believe Janel actually had to deal with the fear of her beloved son dying on the streets because she stopped bringing him food. As irrational as it sounds, I believe the powerful emotion of fear trumps logic every time.

About a month or so after Janel's announcement, she told the group that she had called Ernie and told him that he would not be allowed to come home and take showers anymore. Once again, she reported that Ernie said "Whatever" and hung up. Once again I believe Janel, a loving mother, had to grapple with that unreasonable fear about her son's survival.

After a couple more months of coming to meetings, Janel announced that she told Ernie that he needed to come and get the seven boxes of his personal items that had been stored in her garage for the past ten years. She offered to help him move the boxes and said she would give him thirty days' time to do so or would donate those boxes to Salvation Army. After about another month, she announced to the group Ernie did not come and pick up his stuff and so she did indeed follow through with her commitment and donated the items to the Salvation Army.

I believe Janel had to go through this terrible waiting period again to make sure that Ernie did not die. So, after another month or so, she announced to the group that she called her son and told him that she could not give him any more money for any reason. This time Ernie spouted an expletive and hung up on her.

Now another waiting period had to happen. Would Ernie die with no financial support from his mom? She assumed he would take odd jobs and daily labor to earn money and would panhandle to get money. She also suspected he may have been shoplifting and stealing in order to continue to live his sad, chosen lifestyle.

Janel's Son Gets Help
About a month after Janel cut Ernie's final financial string, she got a phone call from him from jail.

He had been picked up on a drug charge. He also reported, with sadness in his voice, that his friend from the streets had overdosed on heroin and died. Ernie said he was serious now about his recovery and wanted to enter a treatment center upon release from jail. Naturally, Janel was happy to hear this, but she had heard it before. Because of her new learning, she was cautiously optimistic.

A couple of weeks later, Janel got another phone call from Ernie. He was released from jail and sitting in his probation officer's office. He told Janel that, true to his promise, he was on the waiting list of a local county-run drug and alcohol rehab program. It could be a week or two, however, before a bed would be available for him.

So he asked Janel, "Mom, can I come home until a bed opens up at the treatment center?"

Janel later reported to our group that, without a lot of thought, she said, "No." Whereupon Ernie spat out an expletive and hung up the phone.

Janel says that she would never have been able to say "no" without having gone through those previous experiences of gradually cutting those financial strings with her son. She got strength from her courage to make baby-step changes in how she was helping her son.

This is a wonderful example of both baby steps and incremental learning through time and experience. As it turned out, Ernie's probation officer found a halfway house for him, and he lived there for about two weeks and then entered treatment and completed the program successfully.

Janel Today
Janel has experienced Magic Moment #6: Peace. As of this printing, Ernie has been clean and sober for six years. He has a job helping addicts and their families, he has healthy hobbies and healthy friends, and now Janel sees her son as a healthy adult man.

ABOUT THE AUTHOR

Michael Speakman is a Licensed Substance Abuse Counselor with an expertise in Family Education About Addiction. Having worked in treatment centers since 1988, he has a passion for sharing practical knowledge about recovery with family members of addicts and alcoholics. Mike is currently on staff at Calvary Addiction Recovery Center, a faith-based residential treatment center for substance abuse and problem gambling in Phoenix, Arizona.

Mike became interested in the field through his own journey of discovery:

> *My own wake-up call came at age thirty-six. I was married with two children and was experiencing exceptional financial success in my career. I was supposed to be happy but was far from it. I was a miserable person with the self-awareness of a gnat and the self-centeredness of an angry five-year-old.*
>
> *I had emotional issues that were never dealt with and was battling my own addiction issues. My wake-up call came from going through a divorce which led to a suicide attempt. It wasn't that I wanted to die; I just couldn't stand the overwhelming emotional pain I was feeling and could not get it to stop.*
>
> *At the time It felt worse than physical pain, and I had no clue what it was or what I could do to make it go away, other than to end it all. So, my motive for my*

action was to stop the pain. Taking the action of closing my garage door, turning my car engine on, and lying down scared me enough to go into my house, where I was living alone, and calling my sister for help. She gave me the name of a counselor who I went to see, and that began my journey of emotional healing. I had no idea back then that, ten years later, I would be a counselor myself.

In 2006, Mike founded the first PAL Group (Parents of Addicted Loved ones), a no-cost, educational self-help group for parents struggling with the problems of an addicted adult child.

ACKNOWLEDGMENTS

This book would not be possible without the assistance of many wonderful people. I thank them all for being in my life and for inspiring me to write this book either through their direct assistance or their teachings. I could not have done it without them.

First, thanks to my beautiful wife, Karen, for her support, patience, and love. Also a huge thank you to Mary Westheimer for her continued support. Without her, this book would still live in the notebooks on the shelves of my office.

Thanks to my dear family and friends, including Mary and Jeff Yarter, Anne Speakman and Dr. Frank Rasen, Michael D. and LeAnn Speakman, Reece Speakman, Krystina Batt, Travis and Emma Batt, Bob Speakman, Kimberlee and Rex Marsh, Paul and Debbie Kelcher, David Jenny, Steve Easterling, Doug DeMuth, Ken and Barb Sierecki, Hamilton and Sharon Wallace, Leilani and Frank Palmieri, Clyde and Nancy Curnow, George and Delia Staub, Larry Solomon, Lee Cox, Jon George, Bobbe McGinley, Kristen Smith, Mike Finecey, and all the loving, supportive people at Salvation Army and Calvary Addiction Recovery Center. Your care and friendship has helped to make me the person I am today.

Thanks, too, to the dedicated people who read the rough manuscript and made invaluable contributions to its quality. They include Joyce Page, Kim and Michelle Humphrey, Mike Rehm, Elizabeth Marietti, Phyllis Nielson, Nancy Contardi, Deborah Scott, Arlene Rice, Kim Minert, Jeff Bauer, Michelle Ziff, Mike Pinch, Lynn Shields, Will

Klemovage, Steve McIndoo, Diane Buxton, Jeanette Krohne, Cindy Stone, Todd Matthews, Dee Psarros, Alan Sieber, Cathy Dreifort, Edith Pitts, Laurie Fagan, Eric and Sam Page, Alan Regier, Chris Sopa, Ed and Toni Shiles, Catherine Behan, and Laurie Rodgers.

Thanks are also due to the colleagues, clients, and many families I have worked with during the past twenty-five years as well as all of the PAL Group facilitators and the church leaders who provide space for our PAL meetings.

Your undying support of this project has helped to make a difference in thousands of people's lives.

INDEX

Abstinence, 72, 170, 178, 179

Addict, 7, 70, 133, 175

Addict Roles, 10

Addiction, 175

Adult coping skills, 59, 68, 83, 135

Aftercare, 145, 146, 150, 154, 160, 176, 200

After Treatment Options, 131

Alcohol Addict, 7

Baby steps, 53, 85, 133, 216

Behavioral message, 89

Big 5 (ways to show Love), 56

Cardinal rules, 50, 194

Change, 26, 145, 154

Child coping skills, 64

Childish, 58

Childlike, 58

Choices, 94

Codependency, 46, 76, 213

Comfort zone, 87

Consequences, 55, 155, 180, 197

Coping Phase, 11

Cultural blind spot, 63

Delayed emotional growth, 58, 64, 67

Desperation, 11, 111

Detox, 130

Disempowered, 58, 89, 174

Drug abuser, 70

Drug addict, 70
Empowered, 75, 174
Enabling, 44, 49, 69, 76,134, 200
Encouragement, 56
Expectations, 186
Family education, eleven principles of, 91
Financial help, 180, 181, 182
First-timer, 17
Foundation of new knowledge, 25
Friendship, unhealthy, 137
Friendships, in recovery, 138
Full adulthood, 90
Game is up, 15
Gems, 127
Growth pain, 115
Guilt, false, 33, 62, 80, 209
Guilt, true, 33, 62
Halfway house, 131, 152
Healthy helping, 44
Healthy Selfishness, 116
Honeymoon phase, 11
Hope Hotel, 187
Hopelss Highway, 20
Hopelessness, 18, 183
Incremental Learning, 85, 133, 216
Inpatient treatment, 82, 130, 144
Intensive Outpatient Treatment (IOP), 130
Intervention, 71
Letting go, 164, 167
Leverage, 85
Minding your expectations (MYE), 186
Magic moments, 8
Marathon, 24
Metaphoric Model, 96

Mind altering substances, 110, 178
Natural highs, 179
Nuggets, 188
Over-Helping, 43, 102
PAL Group, 186, 188, 198, 199, 206, 207, 211, 217
Parent Roles, 76, 123
Parents' Plan, 107
Precise Help, 48, 102
Partial Hospitalization (PHP), 130
Picking your battles, 75
Prodigal son time, 190
Rate of change, 145
Recovering Person's Plan, 137, 153, 155
Recovery activities, 136
Recovery program, 125
Re-entry, 144, 153
Rehab, 130, 134
Relapse, 16, 134, 145, 169, 174, 176, 179, 186, 195, 201
Relapse triggers, 171
Rescuer, 76
Residential Treatment, 130
Risk of trusting, 20
Rite-of-passage, 59, 62, 67
Role-model, 188
Role-playing, 126
Self-revealing, 21
Sober Living, 131
Sober Living House, 132, 152
Sponsor, 136, 137, 140
Strings, financial, 87, 103, 153, 210, 215
Substance abuser, 176
Support team, 187
Teachable, 163
Teachable moments, 60, 198

Teachable scale, 164
Temptation, 171
Three D's, 65
Three-Quarter House, 131, 152
Three Stages of Addiction, 11
Total Abstinence, 176, 178
Tough Love, 97
Transitional living, 132, 152
Treatment Options, 130
Treatment-wise, 201
Triggers, 124, 171
Trust, 20, 118
Twelve steps, 136
Unhealthy rescuing, 69
United front, 84
Wasted pain, 115
Writing letters, 57

NOTES

NOTES